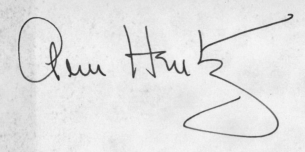

MANUAL OF
HERALDRY

THE
MANUAL OF HERALDRY

A CONCISE DESCRIPTION OF THE
SEVERAL TERMS USED, AND CONTAINING
A DICTIONARY OF EVERY DESIGNATION
IN THE SCIENCE

EDITED BY

FRANCIS J. GRANT

K.C.V.O., LL.D.

ALBANY HERALD

THREE HUNDRED AND FIFTY ILLUSTRATIONS

BARNES & NOBLE, INC.   NEW YORK

PUBLISHERS   •   BOOKSELLERS   •   SINCE 1873

Reprinted .　　. 1962

PRINTED IN GREAT BRITAIN BY
OLIVER AND BOYD LTD., EDINBURGH

PREFACE

THE great revival which has taken place in the study and appreciation of the Science of Heraldry, and the wider and more intelligent interest now taken in armory, has induced the publisher to issue a new and revised edition of this work.

This opportunity has been taken to enlarge and improve the Dictionary of Heraldic Terms, and to cut out much of the repetition which was contained in the opening chapters of the previous editions. The space thus gained has been used to give a larger and, in the light of modern research, more correct view of the Origin of Arms, and to add chapters on the Law and Right to Arms and on the Heraldic Executive.

The chapter formerly given on Precedence has been entirely superseded by inserting the tables now in use in England and in Scotland, and the whole book has been so revised and rewritten as to form practically a new work.

Though in the past the science has suffered much from the absurd and pedantic origins assigned not only to it but to the armorial achievements of various families, its use as an aid to historical research has been long proved and recognised. How often has the date of the foundation of some ancient castle or abbey been discovered or a portrait identified from the armorial bearings thereon, and many an important point in genealogy elucidated, by the charges borne by the individual members of the family explaining their matrimonial alliances, their position as cadets, or even the origin of the house itself.

Preface

Although in the small compass of this volume it has not been found practicable to enter into an elaborate criticism of the various arms used by different families in the United Kingdom, the Editor believes that this *Manual* will be found of service to the student as well as to the general reader who desires to acquire some correct knowledge of what has been justly called "The Shorthand of History."

The Editor is indebted to the late Mr Graham Johnston, Herald Painter in the Lyon Office, for the three illustrations of the royal arms which appear at pages 135, 137, and 139.

CONTENTS

vii

Contents

MANUAL OF HERALDRY

CHAPTER I

ORIGIN OF COATS OF ARMS

HERALDRY is the science which teaches us how to blazon
or describe in proper terms armorial bearings and their
accessories.

Modern writers have long discarded the fabulous origin
attributed by mediæval authors to the assumption of arms.
We now no longer put forward as genuine such arms as
those alleged to belong to Adam and Eve, Noah, Judas
Maccabeus, Pontius Pilate, or even those attributed to
mythical British kings and Anglo-Saxon monarchs before
the Norman Conquest.

In these earlier works on heraldry, the science has
suffered much from the foolish and pedantic attempts
made by the writers to attribute its origin to the Greeks
and Romans, and even to find traces of it in Scripture in
the marks or standards of the tribes of the Children of
Israel. It may safely be stated that its introduction was
coeval with the use of armour in the Middle Ages, when it
became necessary for men to be able to recognise each
other as friend or foe in the *mêlée* of the battle. Thus it
came that warriors adorned their shields with marks to
distinguish each other, and decorated the top of their
helmets with crests.

I

Manual of Heraldry

From the earliest times, however, various symbols, emblems and devices were used on their standards and shields by ancient nations, such as the Greeks and Romans, whose shields were decorated with animals and other objects; and at a later date we have such ensigns as the white horse of the Saxons, the raven of the Norse vikings, the lion of the Normans, and the devices on the shields of the knights depicted in the representation of the Norman Conquest, known as the Bayeux Tapestry. These emblems were, however, not hereditary in families, were changed by their owners at pleasure, and therefore cannot be held to have been heraldic in our modern sense of the word. Similar customs are to be found to this day among such people as the Japanese, and in the totems of the Red Indians and the now extinct Aztecs in North America.

Mr J. R. Planche (*Rouge Croix*) in his book, *The Pursuivant of Arms*, clearly establishes that at the Norman Conquest the use of armorial bearings was quite unknown, and that heraldry appears as a science at the beginning of the thirteenth century, although arms had undoubtedly been borne for some time previous. The evidence both of chroniclers and artists directly disproves any science or practice being in existence at the time of the first and second Crusades.

It is a curious circumstance that our earliest and best examples of heraldry should be due to lack of learning. But for the fact that few persons were able to write and had to authenticate all deeds and transactions they entered on with their seals, we should not now have these records of the earlier armorial ensigns. The practice of sealing dates in England from the time of Edward the Confessor, when the authentication of documents by this means was introduced. These seals were originally not heraldic, and

2

Origin of Coats of Arms

bore various designs, such as equestrian figures, etc., which in turn became decorated with armorial bearings as heraldry came into vogue.

The next authority regarding the early arms of the English nobles and knights is the various rolls or armorials preserved in the Heralds' College, in the British Museum and other public libraries, and in private hands. The earliest of these rolls, which are usually long narrow strips of parchment containing a full description of the arms of the nobles and gentlemen, is dated about 1240, and is in the custody of the College of Arms. One of these written in verse and in Norman-French, known as the Roll of Car-laverock, contains a list of the princes, nobles, bannerets, and knights who formed part of Edward I.'s army at the siege and capture of that castle in Dumfriesshire, in the year 1300, and gives a minute description of their banners and armorial ensigns. This roll has been twice published, first by Sir Harris Nicolas in 1828 and again by Thomas Wright in 1861. These records show that by that time heraldry had been reduced to a system.

Amongst the most valuable records of arms now extant are the visitations made throughout England by various heralds during a period commencing in 1530, and ending with that dated 13th May 1686. These not only contain the armorial bearings, but give detailed pedigrees of the various families.

The most ancient roll of Scottish arms now existing is that contained in the Armorial of Gelre Herald, preserved in the Royal Library at Brussels, and executed about the year 1370, which gives the arms of the King and forty-one coats of Scottish nobles. Another early roll is that of Gilles de Bouvier, Berry King of Arms, preserved in the National Library at Paris, which contains amongst others

Manual of Heraldry

122 Scottish coats. These two rolls have been reproduced by Mr R. R. Stodart in his book on *Scottish Arms*, and the former more correctly by Sir Archibald Dunbar in a paper on the subject printed in the *Proceedings of the Society of Antiquaries of Scotland*, 1890-91.

It is, however, to Sir David Lindsay of the Mount, Lyon King of Arms, we are indebted for the earliest official Register of Scottish Arms, compiled about the year 1542, and at present preserved in the Advocates' Library. This has been twice reproduced in facsimile, first in 1822 by Dr David Laing, and secondly in 1878.

In the thirteenth century the practice of embroidering armorial ensigns on the surcoat worn over a coat of mail gave rise to the expression "coat of arms."

It was at this time that heraldry was to be seen at its best; but by the end of the fourteenth century the true origin of arms had begun to be obscured, and ridiculous and fantastic fables were invented to account for the various charges, and to trace their adoption to the commemoration of supposed adventures and exploits of the ancestors of the owners thereof. From having only simple charges on the escutcheon, the same was gradually crowded with additional objects and even pictorial representations. By the eighteenth century it probably reached its lowest depth in England. In 1760 a grant of arms was made to a family named Tetlow, in Lincolnshire, which included, besides thirteen other charges, a book charged with a silver penny, upon which was written the Lord's Prayer, to commemorate the fact that one of the family had accomplished that feat with a quill pen. Other examples, such as the forty-five feet reflecting telescope of Sir John Herschel's arms, might be quoted, but, with the present revival of interest in the science which began in the latter half of the nineteenth century, it is to be hoped that such degradations are now a thing of the past, though some recent grants of the Heralds' College, such as that to Lord Kitchener, leave much to be desired.

In Scotland, where the number of families is comparatively limited, the necessity of charging the shield with a multitude of objects has never been required, and the debasement of the science fortunately did not extend to the same extent, a circumstance for which perhaps we are indebted to our great writers, Sir George Mackenzie and Alexander Nisbet, who did much to restore heraldry to a sound historical basis. Still, at the beginning of last century during the Peninsula War, several coats granted contained augmentations representing battle scenes, medals, decorations and other unheraldic objects. Probably one of the most curious is that recorded in 1812 for a Mr Bonar, which has, on a chief a dexter hand proper, vested with a shirt sleeve of the first, issuing from the dexter chief point, holding a shoulder of mutton to a lion passant or.

Heraldry does not seem to have reached the Highlands of Scotland before the sixteenth century, and a system of bearing arms prevailed there which was not only crude but bore no reference to the accepted laws of armory. Many of the arms of the various chiefs and gentlemen have quarterings which are in no way indicative of descent or alliance, the arrangement of the quarters being often varied to indicate differences between different clans, certain charges such as the lymphad or galley being common to nearly all those of the West Coast and Islands.

CHAPTER 1I

THE RIGHT TO ARMS

IT is probable that arms were in early times assumed by
the various nobles and gentlemen at their own hand, not
to symbolise (says Mr Planche) "any virtue or qualification
but simply to distinguish their persons and properties, to
display their pretensions to certain honours and estates,
attest their alliances or acknowledge their feudal tenures."
The charges adopted were those that if possible held some
resemblance either in sound or form to the name of the
bearer thereof. As time went on and arms multiplied,
disputes arose between various persons as to their respective
rights to various charges, and their claims were referred to
the arbitration of the King as the fountain of all honour.
As early as 1385 the celebrated case of Scrope *versus*
Grosvenor as to the right to bear the arms, azure a bend or,
was decided in favour of the former by King Richard II.
in person.

It having become necessary that some authority should
be established to regulate the wearing of arms, to preserve
a record of the rights of families to the same, to assign
armorial ensigns to such persons as should be considered
worthy to bear such and to prevent the unwarrantable
assumption of the same, King Richard III. by Royal
Charter in 1483 incorporated the COLLEGE OF ARMS or
HERALDS' COLLEGE, which exercises control over the use of
armorial bearings in England. Similar functions are dis-

The Right to Arms

charged in Scotland by the Court of the Lord Lyon, and in Ireland by the Office of Arms. No arms are of any legal authority or are of any value unless they are recorded in one of these offices.

In England the College of Arms is presided over by the Earl Marshal, and no grant of arms can be made except on a warrant directed by him to Garter, Clarenceux, or Norroy Kings of Arms as the case may be, which warrant proceeds on a petition made to him through one of the officers of arms. The fees of such a grant amount, including a stamp duty of £10, to £76, 10s., and if supporters are included the fee is considerably higher. These charges do not include the fees incurred to the officer of arms by whom the application has been conducted for searches and personal trouble.

THE COURT OF THE LORD LYON in Scotland is one of the judicatures of that country, and all applications therein are conducted in the forms common to other courts of law. The precise date of its origin is not known, but its jurisdiction and the use of armorial bearings are laid down and regulated by a series of Acts of Parliament, the most important of which are those of 1592, cap. 125; 1672, cap. 47; and 30 Victoria, cap. 17, 1867. In this respect armorial law in Scotland differs from that of England.

Petitions to the Lord Lyon for a grant of arms by a *novus homo*, for matriculation by a cadet of a family whose arms are already recorded or for registration of arms borne by one's ancestors before the year 1672, in terms of the statute of that year, may be signed by the petitioner or his counsel or agent. With his petition the applicant will produce the evidence on which he relies to support his pedigree and claim, and whether the application is opposed or not, he must prove his case. Lyon then issues his judgment or interlocutor authorising the Lyon clerk to (1)

Manual of Heraldry

prepare Letters Patent in favour of the petitioner, granting him the Ensigns Armorial therein mentioned; or (2) in the case of a cadet, to matriculate the ancestor's arms of new with the proper difference in the Public Register of All Arms and Bearings in Scotland. These arms can only be borne by the grantee and his eldest son or heir male in perpetuity; all younger sons must by the statutes above mentioned matriculate of new with their proper differences, in contradistinction to the English practice, where cadets add their marks of cadency at their own hand. The various modes of differencing in England and Scotland are described at pages 24 and 26. The fees for a patent of arms amount to about £47, 10s., and for a matriculation about £19, 12s. 6d. If supporters are included in the grant the charges are somewhat higher. An appeal from a judgment of the Lord Lyon will lie to the Inner House of the Court of Session on a question of legal right to a special coat of arms, but not on a question of tinctures or charges.

In Ireland arms are granted by Ulster without the necessity of presenting a formal petition. It is also competent to obtain a confirmation of arms if it can be proved the same have been used for a period of at least 100 years, and the pedigree established for at least three generations. This is not, however, issued as a matter of legal right but of grace, and the arms will be differenced to a certain extent from those previously used. The fees in Ulster's Office are £44 for a grant of arms, £59 with a grant of supporters, and £16 for confirmation of arms.

The Lyon Office in Scotland and the Office of Arms in Ireland are offices under the Crown, and all fees drawn there are paid over to H.M. Treasury, in which respect they differ from the Heralds' College in London, whose revenues are the property of the Corporation.

The Right to Arms

The improper and illegal assumption of arms was prohibited in England from at least the reign of King Henry V. by a proclamation of that monarch, but the English Court of Chivalry, which had jurisdiction in questions of armorial assumption, being practically in abeyance, it has been doubted how far the Courts of Chancery or Common Law have jurisdiction to prevent the wrongful use of arms. In Scotland it is expressly made a statutory offence by the Act of Parliament of 1592, punishable by fine and in certain cases by imprisonment, and the confiscation to the Exchequer of all articles on which the arms may have been placed. This Act has been re-enacted from time to time, and during the eighteenth century numerous prosecutions took place. Though perhaps during last century it has not been so rigorously enforced, the law has been repeatedly put in force to stop the erection of fictitious coats of arms in public places, such as Glasgow Cathedral, M'Ewan Hall in Edinburgh, etc. ; and quite recently the Treasury, acting on the advice of the Lord Advocate, authorised the prosecution of the magistrates of a Scottish Royal Burgh who were using unrecorded arms.

The jurisdiction of the various offices is regulated by the real domicile of the applicant, and not by his temporary residence in one or other country. This rule, however, does not apply to cadets of families whose arms are on record in Scotland, who notwithstanding their place of residence, even though it be in a foreign country, will matriculate their arms in the Lyon Register. Persons residing in British colonies or temporarily in foreign countries will apply to the office of the country of their or their ancestor's origin; but arms will not be granted to persons who are not British subjects.

CHAPTER III

THE HERALDIC EXECUTIVE

THE office of Herald is of more ancient origin than the use of arms, upon which science he has conferred his name.

In all civilised nations heralds were employed at a very early date as messengers of peace or war from the sovereign of one state to another; in the time of chivalry as the arrangers of tournaments, and in more modern times as the superintendents of processions, coronations, state funerals and other public ceremonies, and making royal proclamations; when it became necessary to regulate the use of arms they were the officers to whom the King delegated his authority in these matters. They existed in most European states by the fifteenth century. In France the heralds were formed into an incorporation by King Charles VI. in 1406, under a king of arms called Mountjoy, and under him were ten heralds and pursuivants. In England although the office existed from an early period, it would appear from the fact that no herald or pursuivant is mentioned as taking part in the case of Scrope *versus* Grosvenor in 1385 before referred to, that at that time they had not been entrusted with any jurisdiction in matters armorial. The office of Garter King of Arms was instituted for the service of that order by King Henry V. in 1417, in place of Windsor Herald, by whom the duties were previously performed, and on 5th January 1420 William Bruges was appointed to the office. By this time

The Heraldic Executive

probably the control of Ensigns Armorial had been entrusted to the heralds, and certainly before 1456, when the beautifully illuminated grant of arms was made to the Tallow Chandlers Company of London by John Smert, Garter.

The College of Arms or Heralds' College was not, however, incorporated until 1483, when it received a charter from King Richard III. The college is presided over by the Earl Marshal of England, an office now hereditary in the family of Howard, Duke of Norfolk, under Letters Patent, dated 19th October 1672, in favour of Henry, Lord Howard of Castle Rising, and his heirs of entail. Under him are Garter, principal king of all English arms, and two provincial kings, Surrey, instituted in the reign of King Edward III., whose title was changed to Clarenceux by King Henry V., with jurisdiction south of the river Trent; and Norroy, the most ancient, probably a herald before the reign of Edward II., with jurisdiction over the northern parts of England beyond the said river. There are now six heralds, viz. :—Chester, Windsor, Lancaster, and York, instituted by King Edward III. ; Richmond, by King Edward IV. ; and Somerset, by King Henry VIII. The pursuivants, the lowest degree of officers of arms, are four in number, viz. :—Rouge Croix, called from the red cross of St George in the arms of England; Blue Mantle, from the blue mantle of France assumed by Edward III. ; Rouge Dragon, from the badge of Wales and also from the supporter assumed by Henry VII. ; and Portcullis, from the badge of that monarch. There were also a number of other officers of arms bearing other titles, whose offices are now extinct. Occasionally for such ceremonies as coronations extraordinary heralds and pursuivants are created, as for example at the late King Edward's, Fitzalan Pursuivant;

Manual of Heraldry

and at King George V.'s, Fitzalan and Carnarvon Pursuivants. These officers are absorbed into the ordinary establishment as vacancies occur.

The Scottish officers of arms formed an important part of the Royal Household, and were in attendance on the King on all occasions of state. Besides the duties enumerated above, they were employed in accompanying embassies abroad, making royal proclamation throughout the country, carrying important messages of state between the King and his subjects, and a summons for treason could only be served by a herald or pursuivant.

As early as 1364 mention is made of William Pittolloch, Herald; and in 1365, in the Great Seal Register, of John Trupour, Carrick Herald (probably a mistake for pursuivant). Lyon Herald appears in 1377, and ten years later as Lyon King of Heralds. Rothesay Herald, officer of the Prince of Scotland, is first mentioned in 1401; Marchmont, a title derived from Marchmont, the ancient name of the Royal Castle of Roxburgh, in 1436; Snowdoun, derived from a part of Stirling Castle, in 1448; Albany, from the Duke of Albany, a title of one of the King's sons, in 1451 (he is called pursuivant, however, in 1447); Ross, from the Royal Earldom of the same, in 1474; and Islay, from the island of that name, in 1493. Other heralds are also found from time to time, such as Ireland in 1498 and Orkney in 1581.

Of the pursuivants, Carrick, Pursuivant of the Prince, who was Earl of Carrick, appears first in the year 1365; Unicorn in 1426; Aliszai in 1426; Dragance in 1429; Diligence in 1472; Dingwall in 1479; Montrose, Bute and Ormond in 1488; Falkland in 1493; Ireland and Kintyre in 1495; March in 1515; and Ettrick, "pretendit pursuivant," in 1571.

The number of heralds and pursuivants became fixed at

six of each by the reign of King James VI., and continued at this number till by the Act of 1867 their numbers were gradually reduced to three of each as vacancies occurred. The titles now in use are Ross, Rothesay, and Albany for the heralds; and Unicorn, Falkland, and Carrick for the pursuivants.

The Office of Arms in Ireland is presided over by Ulster King of Arms, an office dating from the year 1552. Under him is a pursuivant named Athlone, who also acts as Registrar of Arms. There are two heralds attached to the Order of St Patrick, called Dublin and Cork.

Garter, Lyon, and Ulster are respectively Kings of Arms of the Orders of the Garter, Thistle, and St Patrick; but there are also Bath, King of Arms of that order, created in 1725, and a King of Arms, without title, of the Order of St Michael and St George.

In England the kings of arms, heralds, and pursuivants are appointed by the Crown, and in Scotland Lyon and Lyon clerk are similarly appointed; but the heralds and pursuivants received their commissions from Lyon.

The official dress of an officer of arms is called a tabard, which is a surcoat bearing the Royal Arms on the front, back, and sleeves. That of a king of arms is made of velvet, of a herald of satin, and of a pursuivant of flowered damask silk. At coronations a king of arms wears a crown of gold formed of acanthus leaves rising out of a circlet, upon which is this inscription, " Miserere mei Dominus secundum tuam miserecordiam "; but on other occasions, in common with the other officers of arms, a black velvet cap whereon is embroidered a rose, thistle, or shamrock, ensigned with a royal crown according to nationality. Kings of arms and heralds have further a collar of S.S., the former being of gold and the latter of silver.

Manual of Heraldry

While on the Continent there does not exist any institution similar to the heraldic authorities in this country, there is in Germany, Austria, Russia, Belgium, and Holland, through the various chanceries of the orders of knighthood, a direct supervision of arms. In Norway and Sweden, where titles of nobility have been abolished, armorial ensigns are still regulated in the same manner; but in republics such as France and the United States there is no supervision in those matters. Persons in the British Colonies will apply for grants or matriculation of arms to the authority of the country of their origin.

There is an extraordinary popular delusion exemplified on the stage and in pictures that a herald carries a trumpet, which he sounds before proclaiming. It was difficult to understand how this arose, but probably it had its origin in the fact that on certain occasions he was accompanied by a Royal Trumpeter and the offices were confused.

In the times of chivalry many of the great nobles had heralds and pursuivants attached to their household whose surcoats bore their lords' arms, but their duties were not armorial.

CHAPTER IV

Arms of Dominion, Pretension, Concession, Community, Patronage, Family, Alliance, and Succession

Arms of Dominion or Sovereignty are properly the arms of the kings or sovereigns of the territories they govern, which are also regarded as the arms of the State. Thus the Lions of England and the Russian Eagle are the arms of the Kings of England and the Emperors of Russia, and cannot properly be altered by a change of dynasty.

Arms of Pretension are those of kingdoms, provinces, or territories to which a prince or lord has some claim, and which he adds to his own, though the kingdoms or territories are governed by a foreign king or lord: thus the Kings of England for many ages quartered the arms of France in their escutcheon as the descendants of Edward III., who claimed that kingdom, in right of his mother, a French princess.

Arms of Concession are arms granted by sovereigns as the reward of virtue, valour, or extraordinary service. All arms granted to subjects were originally conceded by the Sovereign.

Arms of Community are those of bishoprics, cities, universities, academies, societies, and corporate bodies.

Arms of Patronage are such as governors of provinces, lords of manors, etc., add to their family arms as a token of their superiority, right, and jurisdiction.

Manual of Heraldry

Arms of Family, or paternal arms, are such as are hereditary and belong to one particular family, which none others have a right to assume, nor can they do so without rendering themselves guilty of a breach of the laws of honour punishable by the Earl Marshal and the Kings at Arms.

Arms of Alliance are those gained by marriage.

Arms of Succession are such as are taken up by those who inherit certain estates by bequest, entail, or donation.

Arms of Affection are such as have been assumed out of gratitude to a benefactor, being quartered with the paternal arms. An example of this will be found in the coat of Boyle, Earl of Glasgow, who bears the arms of Boyle, Earl of Burlington, quarterly with the arms of the earldom, as a mark of affection.

SHIELDS, TINCTURES, FURS, ETC.

The *Shield* contains the field or ground whereon are represented the charges or figures that form a coat of arms. These were painted on the shield before they were placed on banners, standards, and coat armour; and wherever they appear at the present time they are painted on a plane or superficies resembling a shield.

Shields in heraldic language are called Escutcheons or Scutcheons, from the Latin word *scutum*. The forms of the

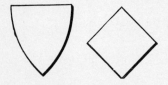 shield or field upon which arms are emblazoned are varied according to the taste of the painter. The Norman pointed shield is generally used in heraldic paintings in ecclesiastical buildings : the escutcheons of maiden ladies and widows are painted on a lozenge-shaped shield. Armorists distinguish several points in the escutcheon

Tinctures

in order to determine exactly the position of the bearings or charges. They are denoted in the annexed diagram, by the first nine letters of the alphabet ranged in the following manner:—

A, the dexter chief.
B, the middle chief.
C, the sinister chief.
D, the honour point.
E, the fess point.
F, the nombril point.
G, the dexter base.
H, the middle base.
I, the sinister base.

The dexter side of the escutcheon answers to the left hand, and the sinister side to the right hand of the person who looks at it.

TINCTURES

By the term *Tincture* is meant that variable hue which is given to shields and their bearings; they are divided into metals, colours, and furs.

These colours are denoted in engravings by various lines or dots, a system invented by an Italian in the beginning of the seventeenth century, as follows:—

OR, which signifies *gold*, and in colour yellow, is expressed by dots.

ARGENT signifies *silver* or *white*: it is left quite plain.

Manual of Heraldry

 GULES signifies *red:* it is expressed by lines drawn from the chief to the base of the shield.

 AZURE signifies *blue:* it is represented by lines drawn from the dexter to the sinister side of the shield, parallel to the chief.

 VERT signifies *green:* it is represented by slanting lines, drawn from the dexter to the sinister side of the shield.

 PURPURE, or *purple*, is expressed by diagonal lines, drawn from the sinister to the dexter side of the shield.

 SABLE, or *black*, is expressed by horizontal and perpendicular lines crossing each other.

 TENNE, which is *tawny*, or *orange* colour, is marked by diagonal lines drawn from the sinister to the dexter side of the shield, traversed by perpendicular lines from the chief.

Furs

 Sanguine is *dark red*, or *murrey* colour: it is represented by diagonal lines crossing each other.

These last two tinctures are not of common occurrence.

In addition to the foregoing tinctures, there are ten roundels or balls used in armory, the names of which are sufficient to denote their colour without expressing the same. For these charges, see under the following titles in the Dictionary, viz.:—Bezant, Fountain, Golpe, Guzes, Hurts, Orange, Pellet, Plate, Pomeis, and Torteaux.

Furs

Furs are used to ornament garments of state and denote dignity: they are used in heraldry, not only for the lining of mantles of sovereigns and peers and other ornaments of the shield, but also as tinctures on escutcheons.

White, represented by a plain shield, like argent.

 Ermine, white powdered with black tufts.

 Ermines, field sable, powdering argent.

 Erminois, field or, powdering sable.

19

PEAN, field sable, powdering or.

VAIR, argent and azure. It is represented by small bells, part reversed, ranged in lines in such a manner that the base argent is opposite to the base azure.

COUNTER-VAIR, is when the bells are placed base against base, and point against point.

POTENT, an obsolete word for a crutch: it is so called in Chaucer's description of Old Age.

> " So eld she was that she ne went
> A foote, but it were by potent."

The field is filled with small potents, ranged in lines, azure and argent.

POTENT COUNTER-POTENT, the heads of the crutches or potents touch each other in the centre of the shield.

CHAPTER V

ESCUTCHEONS of more than one tincture are divided by lines. When the line is perpendicular, it is called per pale; horizontal, per fess; diagonal line from dexter, per bend; diagonal line sinister, per bend sinister; and so forth.

When a line is not simple and straight, it has an heraldic name expressive of its form. The following are the names of the principal modifications of straight lines used in British heraldry:—

Engrailed . . .

Invected . . .

Wavy, or undé . . .

Embattled, or crenelle . .

Nebule . . . .

Indented . . .

Dancetté . . .

21

Manual of Heraldry

Angled . . . .

Bevilled . . .

Escartelle . . . .

Nowy, or franché . .

Dovetailed . . . .

Embattled grady: sometimes called battled embattled . .

Potent . . . .

Double arched . . .

Arched, or enarched . .

Urdée . . . .

Radiant . . . .

If a shield is divided into four equal parts, it is said to be quartered.

QUARTERED PER CROSS.—The shield is divided into four parts, called quarters, by an horizontal and perpendicular line, crossing each other in the centre of the field, each of which is numbered. These quarters may in turn be themselves quartered, and when this is the case the leading quarters are called GRAND QUARTERS, and are said to be quarterly quartered.

The escutcheon may be thus subdivided into a great many parts, the shield of Mr Henry Crampton Lloyd, of Stockton-on-Cherbury, Salop, bearing no less than 356 quarters. When the number of coats to which a person may be entitled is an odd number, the last quarter is filled up by repeating the first. In practice, however, it is better to limit the number of quarterings, for when the coats are numerous, the charges become so small as to be not easily distinguishable.

DIFFERENCES OR BRISURES

All members of the same family claim the same bearings in their coat of arms; and to distinguish the principal bearer from his descendants or relatives, it was necessary to invent some sign, so that the degree of consanguinity might be known. These signs are called DIFFERENCES. During the Crusades the only difference consisted in the bordure or border, which, as the name implies, was a border or edging running round the edge of the shield. The colour and form of this border served to distinguish the leaders of the different bands that served under one duke or chieftain.

The same difference might be used to de-
note a diversity between particular persons descended from one family. At the present time, in England, they are not used to denote a difference, but as one of the ordinaries to a coat of arms. The annexed example exhibits the arms of the Monastery of Bermondsey. Party per pale, azure and gules; a bordure, argent. This bordure

is plain; but they may be formed by any of the fore-going lines.

The annexed example is or, a bordure engrailed, gules.

The differences used by heralds in England, and to a certain extent in Scotland, at the present time, are nine in number. They not only distinguish the sons of one family, but also denote the subordinate degrees in each house.

The Heir, or first son, the LABEL . .

Second Son, the CRESCENT . . .

Third Son, the MULLET . , .

Fourth Son, the MARTLET . , .

Fifth Son, the ANNULET . .

Sixth Son, the FLEUR-DE-LIS '. . .

Differences

Seventh Son, the ROSE   .   .   .

Eighth Son, the CROSS MOLINE   .   .

Ninth Son, the DOUBLE QUATREFOIL   .

Should either of the nine brothers have male children, the eldest child would place the label on the difference that distinguished his father; the second son would place the crescent upon it; the third the mullet; continuing the same order for as many sons as he may have.

The label only is used in the arms of the royal family as a difference; but the points of the label are charged with different figures to distinguish the second and succeeding sons. The arms of the Prince of Wales are distinguished by a label of three points argent; of the Duke of Connaught by a label, the centre point charged with St George's Cross and each of the other points with a fleur-de-lis azure; the Duke of Albany, the centre point with St George's Cross and the others with a heart gules; and the Duke of Cumberland, the centre point charged with a fleur-de-lis argent and the others with a St George's Cross.

All the figures denoting differences are also used as perfect charges on the shield; but their size and situation will sufficiently determine whether the figure is used as a perfect coat of arms, or is introduced as a difference or diminution.

Manual of Heraldry

In Scotland, by statute, all younger sons and cadets being obliged to re-register the family arms, with their proper differences, the usual manner of so doing is by bordure, which is again further differenced among the younger sons of younger sons by being engrailed, invected, indented, embattled, and so forth, as will be seen from the plate showing the scheme of difference at present used in the Court of the Lord Lyon. The compulsory matriculation of arms by cadets ensures that the heraldry of the family is maintained on a proper basis, and not, as in England, left to the will of the individuals themselves; and also indicates their position in the family for many more generations than is possible by using single charges.

Sisters have no differences in their coats of arms. They are permitted to bear the arms of their father, as the eldest son does after his father's decease.

Guillim, Leigh, and other ancient armorists mention divers figures, which, they assert, were formerly added to coats of arms as marks of degradation for slander, cowardice, murder, and other crimes, and to them they give the name of abatements of honour; others have called them blots in the escutcheon; but as no instance can be produced of such dishonourable marks having been borne in a coat of arms, they may justly be considered as chimerical, or at any rate obsolete, and unworthy of consideration at the present time. Porney pithily observes "that arms being marks of honour, they cannot admit of any note of infamy, nor would any one bear them if they were so branded." It is true a man may be degraded for divers crimes, particularly high treason; but in such cases the escutcheon was reversed, trod upon, and torn in pieces, and the entry of his arms in the official registers deleted, to denote a total extinction and suppression of the honour and dignity of

26

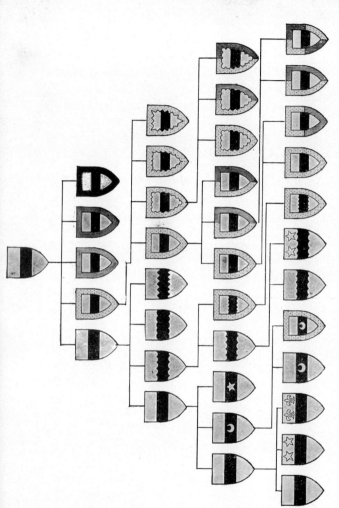

THE SCHEME OF CADENCY OR DIFFERENCING IN SCOTLAND.

[To face p. 26.

Differences

the person to whom it belonged. Examples of such proceedings may be seen in the deletion of the arms of the Earl of Gowrie in 1600 in Sir Robert Forman's Register, and also in the Lyon Register of the arms of Covenanters, in the reign of King Charles II., who had been forfeited.

The only abatements used in heraldry are those for illegitimacy, which is denoted in England by a baton sinister, and in Scotland by a bordure compony. Examples of this will be found in the escutcheons of certain peers who assume the royal arms as the illegitimate descendants of King Charles the Second and King William the Fourth.

The charges in heraldry may be said to include almost every object on the earth or in the heavens or under the sea. The most common of these will be found in the Dictionary, where, however, it has not been considered necessary to mention objects which are the same as those in common use, unless there is some difference in heraldry.

There are certain divisions of charges made by writers on heraldry which have not been followed, for the sake of brevity in a work of this size. The principal of these divisions are what are called the Ordinaries and Sub-Ordinaries. These will be found under their respective headings in the Dictionary.

The External Ornaments of Escutcheons

The ornaments that accompany or surround escutcheons were introduced to denote the birth, dignity, or office of the person to whom the coat of arms belongs. We shall merely give the names of the various objects in this place, and refer the reader to the different words in the Dictionary.

Manual of Heraldry

Over regal escutcheons are placed the crown which pertains to the nation over which the sovereign presides. The crown is generally surmounted with a crest: as in the arms of the kings of England from the time of Edward III. the crown is surmounted by a lion statant, guardant, crowned, and that of the King of Scotland with a lion sejant affrontee.

Over the papal arms is placed a tiara or triple crown, without a crest.

Above the arms of archbishops and bishops the mitre is placed instead of a crest.

Coronets are worn by all princes and peers. They vary in form according to the rank of the nobleman. A full description will be found in the Dictionary of the coronets of the Prince of Wales, royal dukes, dukes, marquises, earls, viscounts, and barons.

Helmets are placed over arms, and show the rank of the person to whom the arms belong: (1) by the metal of which they are made; (2) by their form; (3) by their position. See the word HELMET in the Dictionary.

Mantlings were possibly the ancient coverings of helmets, to preserve them and the bearers from the injuries of the weather, or to keep the head of the wearer from getting too heated by the rays of the sun. They are now formed into scroll-work proceeding from the sides of the helmet, and are great ornaments to an escutcheon. See a more full description under the word MANTLING.

A *chapeau* is an ancient hat or rather cap of dignity worn by dukes. They were formed of scarlet velvet and turned up with fur. They are frequently used instead of a wreath under the crests of noblemen and even gentlemen.

The *wreath* was formed by two large skeins of silk of

28

External Ornaments

different colours twisted together. This was worn at the lower part of the crest, as a means of fastening it to the helmet. In heraldry the wreath appears like a roll of two colours composed of the principal metal and principal colour appearing on the shield. The crest is usually placed upon the wreath.

The *crest* is the highest part among the ornaments of a coat of arms. It is called crest from the Latin word *crista*, which signifies comb or tuft.

Crests were used as marks of honour long before the introduction of heraldry. The helmets and crests of the Greek and Trojan warriors are beautifully described by Homer. Their use as armorial bearings, however, was of later date than the introduction of arms, the earliest example being found in 1198 in the lion upon the head-dress of Geoffrey, Count of Anjou. From the fact that families have frequently varied and changed their crests, and that many different families have the same charge, a crest is not of equal importance to the shield from a heraldic point of view, notwithstanding the popular idea to the contrary. Many modern crests such as a sun shining on a sunflower, or a hand pointing to a celestial crown, could not possibly have been worn in the days of chivalry, from the impossibility of wearing such objects on a helmet. The custom of bearing more than one crest is illogical, as a person has only one head, and therefore could not wear two helmets. Crests further should not, as is common in crest brooches, be surrounded by a garter, that being the exclusive right of knights of that order. The German heralds pay great attention to crests, and depict them as towering to a great height above the helmet. Knights who were desirous of concealing their rank, or wished particularly to distinguish themselves either in the battlefield or tourney, frequently decorated their helmets with plants or flowers, chimerical figures, animals, etc.; these badges were also assumed by their descendants. The scroll is a label or ribbon containing the motto: it is usually placed in England beneath the shield and supporters, and in Scotland above the crest; see the word MOTTO in the Dictionary.

CHAPTER VI

THE symbolic figures of heraldry are so well known to those acquainted with the science in every kingdom of Europe, that if an Englishman was to send a written emblazonment or description of an escutcheon to a French, German, or Spanish artist acquainted with the English language, either of them could return a properly drawn and coloured escutcheon; but a correct emblazonment would be indispensable. A single word omitted would spoil the shield.

I

It may be necessary to inform the reader that in em-blazoning an escutcheon, the colour of the field is first named; then the principal ordinary, such as the fess, the chevron, etc., naming the tincture and form of the ordinary; then proceed to describe the charges on the field, naming their situation, metal, or colour; lastly, describe the charges on the ordinary.

II

When an honourable ordinary or some one figure is placed upon another, whether it be a fess, chevron, cross, etc., it is always to be named after the ordinary or figure over which it is placed, with either the words surtout or over all.

III

In the blazoning such ordinaries as are plain, the bare mention of them is sufficient; but if an ordinary should be formed of any of the curved or angular lines, such as invected, indented, etc., the lines must be named.

IV

When a principal figure possesses the centre of the field, its position is not to be expressed; it is always understood to be in the middle of the shield.

V

When the situation of a principal bearing is not expressed, it is always understood to occupy the centre of the field. *Ex*. See Azure, an annulet argent (p. 54).

VI

The number of the points of mullets must be specified if more than five: also if a mullet or any other charge is pierced, it must be mentioned.

VII

When a ray of the sun or other single figure is borne in any other part of the escutcheon than the centre, the point it issues from must be named.

VIII

The natural colour of trees, plants, fruits, birds, etc., is to be expressed in emblazoning by the word *proper ;* but if they vary from their natural colour, the tincture or metals that is used must be named.

Marshalling Charges on Escutcheons

IX

Two metals or two colours cannot be put one over the other: thus or cannot be placed on argent or gules on azure.

X

When there are many figures of the same species borne in coats of arms, their number must be observed as they stand, and properly expressed. The annexed arrangements of roundels in shields will show how they are placed and described.

The two roundels are arranged in pale, but they may appear in chief or base: or in fess, as in No. 2.

Three roundels, two over one; if the single roundel had been at the top, it would have been called *one over two*.

Three roundels in bend. They might also be placed in fess, chief, base, or in pale.

Manual of Heraldry

 Four roundels, two over two. Some writers call them *cantoned*, as they form a square figure.

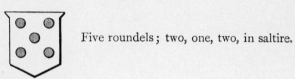 Five roundels; two, one, two, in saltire.

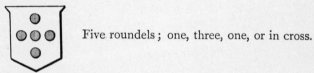 Five roundels; one, three, one, or in cross.

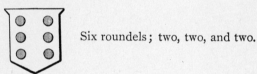 Six roundels; two, two, and two.

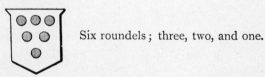 Six roundels; three, two, and one.

There are seldom more figures than seven; but no matter the number, they are placed in the same way,

Marshalling Charges on Escutcheons

commencing with the figures at the top of the shield, or in chief. If the field is strewed all over with roundels, this will be expressed by the word *semée*.

Marshalling coats of arms is the act of disposing the arms of several persons in one escutcheon, so that their relation to each other may be clearly marked.

In heraldry, the husband and wife are called *baron and femme;* and when they are descended from distinct families, both their arms are placed in the same escutcheon, divided by a perpendicular line through the centre of the shield. As this line runs in the same direction, and occupies part of the space in the shield appropriated to the ordinary called the pale, the shield is in heraldic language said to be *parted per pale*. The arms of the baron (the husband) are always placed on the dexter side of the escutcheon; and the femme (the wife) on the sinister side, as in the annexed example.

 Parted per pale, baron and femme, two coats; first, or, a chevron gules; second, barry of twelve pieces, azure and argent.

If a widower marries again, the arms of both his wives are placed on the sinister side, which is parted per fess; that is, parted by an horizontal line running in the direction of the fess, and occupying the same place. The arms of the first wife are placed in the upper compartment of the shield, called the chief; the arms of the second wife in the lower compartment, called the base. This practice, however, is not usual, and the husband usually impales the arms of the second wife alone.

Manual of Heraldry

Ex. Parted per pale, baron and femme, three coats:—first, gules, on a bend argent, three trefoils vert: second, parted per fess, in chief azure, a mascle or, with a label argent for difference. In base ermine, a fess, dancette gules. The same rule would apply if the husband had three or more wives; they would all be placed in the sinister division of the shield; but in none of these cases do the arms descend to the children.

Where the husband marries an heiress, he does not impale his arms with hers, as in the preceding examples, but bears them in an escutcheon of pretence in the centre of the shield, showing his pretension to her arms in consequence of his marriage with the lady who is legally entitled to them. The escutcheon of pretence is not used by the children of such marriage; they bear the arms of their father and mother quarterly, and so transmit them to posterity. Annexed is an example of the arms of the wife on escutcheon of pretence.

Baron and femme, two coats; first, gules, a saltire argent; second, on an escutcheon of pretence, azure, a chevron, or.

If a peeress in her own right marries a private gentleman, their coats of arms are not conjoined paleways, as baron and femme, but are placed upon separate shields by the side of each other; they are sometimes inclosed in a mantle, the shield of the husband occupying the dexter side of the mantle, that of the wife the sinister; each party has a right to all the ornaments incidental to their rank. The husband, who only ranks as an esquire, has no right

Marshalling Charges on Escutcheons

to supporters or coronet, but exhibits the proper helmet, wreath, and crest.

The peeress, by marrying one beneath her in rank, confers no dignity on her husband, but loses none of her own. She is still addressed as "your ladyship," though her husband only ranks as a gentleman; and it is for this reason that the arms cannot be conjoined in one shield as baron and femme.

Ex. Baron and femme, two achievements.

First, azure, a pile or, crest a star of six points, argent; second, gules, a cross flory argent, surmounted by an

earl's coronet: supporters, on the dexter side a stag ducally gorged and chained, on the sinister side a griffin gorged and chained, both proper; motto, Honour and Truth.

In the arms of the wife joined to the paternal coat of the husband, the proper differences borne by the father of the lady must be inserted.

If the coat of the husband has a bordure, that must be omitted on the sinister side of the palar line.

Archbishops and bishops of the Church of England

impale their paternal arms with the arms of the see over which they preside, placing the arms of the bishopric on the dexter, and their paternal arms on the sinister side of the shield; a bishop does not emblazon the arms of his wife on the same shield with that which contains the arms of the see, but on a separate shield.

Arms of augmentation are marshalled according to the direction of the heraldic authorities; they may be placed on a canton in the dexter chief of the shield; in some cases they occupy the whole of the chief, or may take the form of quarterings. The mark of distinction denoting a baronet of England and Great Britain and the United Kingdom is usually placed on an escutcheon, on the fess point of the shield. Baronets of Nova Scotia either place their badges in a canton or suspend them by a tawny ribbon from the shield.

Knights of the various orders, who by the statutes thereof are entitled to encircle their arms with the collars and insignia, do not surround the shield on which they impale their arms with those of their wives with the same, but bear two shields, the dexter bearing their own arms surrounded with their orders, and the sinister a shield impaling the arms of husband and wife, the shield being encircled with a wreath of laurel.

Funeral Escutcheons or Hatchments contain the arms of a deceased person within a black lozenge-shaped frame, and placed over the principal entrance to his house for a period usually about a year after the decease, when they were often placed in churches. The practice is not now so common as formerly, and is seldom now seen in Scotland, where it was usual to surround the escutcheon with the seize quartiers of the deceased. The only difference, as will be seen by the annexed examples, is that the ground of the hatchment is black that surrounds

Marshalling Charges on Escutcheons

the arms of the deceased, whether baron or femme, and white round the arms of the survivor.

In Fig. 1 the black is left on the dexter side, showing that the husband is deceased, and that his wife survives him.

Fig. 2 shows that the husband survives the wife.

Fig. 3 shows that the husband and his first wife are deceased, and that the second wife is the survivor.

Fig. 4. The shield on the dexter side of the hatchment is parted per pale; first, the arms of the bishopric; second, the paternal arms of the bishop. The shield on the sinister side is the arms of the bishop impaling those of his wife as baron and femme; the ground of the hatch-

Manual of Heraldry

ment is black round the sinister side of this shield, showing
that it is the wife that is dead.

Fig. 5 is the hatchment of a lady that
has died unmarried. The arms of
females of all ranks are placed in a
lozenge-shaped shield.

5

Fig. 6 is the hatchment of the widow of a bishop; the
arms are the same as those displayed at Fig. 4: here the

lozenge-shaped shield is parted per
pale. Baron and femme : — first,
parted paleways, on the dexter side
the arms of the bishopric, on the
sinister side the paternal arms of the
bishop. Second, the arms of the
femme; the widow of a bishop has a
right to exhibit the arms of the see

6

over which her husband presided, as, though his death has
dissolved all connection with the see, she has a right to
emblazon all that will honour her deceased husband.

The frame was sometimes ornamented with skull and
cross-bones, and powdered with tears.

For banners, pennons, guidons, etc., and all other matters
where heraldic emblazonment is used in funeral processions,
the reader is referred to the Dictionary.

CHAPTER VII

THE order of precedency to be observed in England was settled by an Act of Parliament passed in the thirty-first year of the reign of Henry VIII. The order has been varied at different periods to accord with the alterations in the families of the reigning monarchs, and the creation of new offices. The following tables show the order of precedency at the present time:—

TABLE OF PRECEDENCY AMONG MEN IN ENGLAND

The SOVEREIGN.
The PRINCE OF WALES.

Younger Sons of the Sovereign.
Grandsons of the Sovereign.
Brothers of the Sovereign.
Uncles of the Sovereign.
The Sovereign's Brothers' or Sisters' Sons (according to the seniority of their parents).
The Archbishop of Canterbury, Lord Primate of All England.
The Lord High Chancellor, or Lord Keeper.
The Archbishop of York, Primate of England.
The Prime Minister.
The Lord Chancellor of Ireland.
The Lord High Treasurer.
The Lord President of the Privy Council.
The Speaker of the House of Commons.
The Lord Privy Seal.
The Lord Great Chamberlain.
The Lord High Constable. ⎫
The Earl Marshal. ⎪ Above
The Lord High Admiral. ⎬ Peers of
The Lord Steward of His Majesty's Household. ⎪ their own
The Lord Chamberlain of His Majesty's Household. ⎭ degree.

Manual of Heraldry

The Master of Horse.

DUKES, according to their Patents of Creation, England, Scotland, Great Britain, Ireland, United Kingdom, and of Ireland since 1801.

Eldest Sons of Dukes of the Royal Blood.

MARQUESSES, according to their Patents of Creation, England, Scotland, Great Britain, Ireland, United Kingdom, and of Ireland since the Union.

Dukes' eldest Sons.

EARLS, according to their Patents as aforesaid.

Younger Sons of Dukes of Blood Royal.

Marquesses' eldest Sons.

Dukes' younger Sons.

VISCOUNTS, according to their Patents as aforesaid.

Earls' eldest Sons.

Marquesses' younger Sons.

Bishops of London, Durham, and Winchester.

All other English Bishops, according to their seniority of consecration.

Secretaries of State and Chief Secretary to Lord-Lieutenant of Ireland, if of the degree of a Baron.

BARONS, according to their Patents as aforesaid.

Lords of Appeal in Ordinary.

Commissioner of the Great Seal.

Treasurer of His Majesty's Household.

Comptroller of His Majesty's Household.

Vice-Chamberlain of His Majesty's Household.

Secretaries of State and Chief Secretary to Lord-Lieutenant of Ireland under the degree of Barons.

Viscounts' eldest Sons.

Earls' younger Sons.

Barons' eldest Sons.

Knights of the Most Noble Order of The Garter.

Knights of St Patrick.

Privy Councillors.

Chancellor of the Exchequer.

Chancellor of the Duchy of Lancaster.

Lord Chief Justice of England.

Master of the Rolls.

The Lords Justices of the Court of Appeal, and President of the Probate, Divorce, and Admiralty Divisions, according to their seniority and order of appointment.

Judges of the High Court of Justice rank among themselves according to date of appointment.

Order of Precedency

Viscounts' younger Sons.

Barons' younger Sons.

Sons of Lords of Appeal in Ordinary (Life Peers), according to seniority of creation.

Baronets of England, Scotland, and Ireland.

Knights Grand Cross of the Bath.

Knights Grand Commanders of the Star of India.

Knights Grand Cross of St Michael and St George.

Knights Grand Commanders of the Order of the Indian Empire.

Knights Grand Cross of the Royal Victorian Order.

Knights Grand Cross of the Order of the British Empire.

Knights Commanders of the Bath.

Knights Commanders of the Star of India.

Knights Commanders of St Michael and St George.

Knights Commanders of the Order of the Indian Empire.

Knights Commanders of the Royal Victorian Order.

Knights Commanders of the Order of the British Empire.

Knights Bachelors.

Judges of County Courts in England and Wales and of City of London Court.

Serjeants-at-Law.

Masters in Lunacy.

Companions of the Bath.

Companions of the Star of India.

Companions of St Michael and St George.

Companions of the Indian Empire.

Commanders of the Royal Victorian Order.

Commanders of the Order of the British Empire.

Companions of the Distinguished Service Order.

Members of the 4th Class of the Royal Victorian Order.

Officers of the Order of the British Empire.

Companions of the Imperial Service Order.

Eldest Sons of the younger Sons of Peers.

Baronets' eldest Sons.

Eldest Sons of Knights of the Garter.

Eldest Sons of Knights Bachelors.

Members of the 5th Class of the Royal Victorian Order.

Members of the Order of the British Empire.

Baronets' younger Sons.

Younger Sons of Knights.

Esquires.

Gentlemen.

Manual of Heraldry

The Queen.

The Queen Dowager.

The Princess of Wales.

Princesses, Daughters of the Sovereign.

Princesses and Duchesses, Wives of the Sovereign's Sons.

Granddaughters of the Sovereign.

Wives of the Sovereign's Grandsons.

The Sovereign's Sisters.

Wives of the Sovereign's Brothers.

The Sovereign's Aunts.

Wives of the Sovereign's Uncles.

Daughters of Dukes of the Blood Royal.

Wives of the Sovereign's Nephews.

Granddaughters of Sovereign not bearing style of Royal Highness.

Duchesses of England, Scotland, Great Britain, Ireland, and United Kingdom.

Wives of the eldest Sons of Dukes of the Blood Royal.

Marchionesses of England, Scotland, Great Britain, Ireland, and United Kingdom.

Wives of the eldest Sons of Dukes.

Daughters of Dukes.

Countesses of England, Scotland, Great Britain, Ireland, and United Kingdom.

Wives of younger Sons of Dukes of Blood Royal.

Wives of the eldest Sons of Marquesses.

Daughters of Marquesses.

Wives of the younger Sons of Dukes.

Viscountesses of England, Scotland, Great Britain, Ireland, and United Kingdom.

Wives of the eldest Sons of Earls.

Daughters of Earls.

Wives of the younger Sons of Marquesses.

Baronesses of England, Scotland, Great Britain, Ireland, and United Kingdom.

Wives of Lords of Appeal in Ordinary (Life Peers), according to seniority of creation of title.

Wives of the eldest Sons of Viscounts.

Daughters of Viscounts.

Wives of the younger Sons of Earls.

Wives of the eldest Sons of Barons.

Order of Precedency

Dame Commanders of the Order of the British Empire.
Daughters of Barons.
Maids of Honour.
Wives of Knights of the Garter.
Wives of Knights of St Patrick.
Wives of the younger Sons of Viscounts.
Wives of the younger Sons of Barons.
Daughters of Lords of Appeal in Ordinary (Life Peers).
Wives of Sons of Lords of Appeal in Ordinary (Life Peers).
Wives of Baronets.
Wives of Knights Grand Cross of the Order of the Bath.
Wives of Knights Grand Commanders of the Star of India.
Wives of Knights Grand Cross of St Michael and St George.
Wives of Knights Grand Commanders of the Order of the Indian Empire.
Wives of Knights Grand Cross of the Royal Victorian Order.
Wives of Knights Grand Cross of the Order of the British Empire.
Wives of Knights Commanders of the Order of the Bath.
Wives of Knights Commanders of the Star of India.
Wives of Knights Commanders of St Michael and St George.
Wives of Knights Commanders of the Indian Empire.
Wives of Knights Commanders of the Royal Victorian Order.
Wives of Knights Commanders of the Order of the British Empire.
Wives of Knights Bachelors.
Commanders of the Order of the British Empire.
Wives of Companions of the Bath.
Wives of Companions of the Star of India.
Wives of Companions of St Michael and St George.
Wives of Companions of the Indian Empire.
Wives of Commanders of the Royal Victorian Order.
Wives of Commanders of the Order of the British Empire.
Wives of Companions of the Distinguished Service Order.
Officers of the Order of the British Empire.
Wives of Members of the 4th Class of the Royal Victorian Order.
Wives of Officers of the Order of the British Empire.
Companions of the Imperial Service Order.
Wives of Companions of the Imperial Service Order.
Wives of the eldest Sons of the younger Sons of Peers.
Daughters of the younger Sons of Peers.
Wives of the eldest Sons of Baronets.
Daughters of Baronets.
Wives of the eldest Sons of Knights of the Garter.

Wives of the eldest Sons of Knights Bachelors.
Daughters of Knights Bachelors.
Members of the Order of the British Empire.
Wives of Members of the 5th Class of the Royal Victorian Order.
Wives of Members of the Order of the British Empire.
Wives of Members of the Imperial Service Order.
Wives of the younger Sons of the younger Sons of Peers.
Wives of the younger Sons of Baronets.
Wives of the younger Sons of Knights.
Wives of Esquires.
Wives of Gentlemen.

THE SCALE OF GENERAL PRECEDENCE IN SCOTLAND

According to Royal Warrant of 9th March 1905

The SOVEREIGN.

The Lord High Commissioner to the General Assembly of the Church of Scotland during the sitting of the General Assembly.

Duke of Rothesay.

Younger Sons of the Sovereign.

Grandsons of the Sovereign.

Brothers of the Sovereign.

Uncles of the Sovereign.

Nephews of the Sovereign.

Note.

Lords Lieutenant of Counties.

Lord Provosts of Cities being *ex officio* Lords Lieutenant of Counties of Cities.

Sheriffs Principal

during their term of office, and within the bounds of their respective Counties, Cities, and Sheriffdoms, shall have precedence next after the Royal Family and the Lord High Commissioner.

Every Lord Lieutenant of a County and every Lord Lieutenant of a County of a City during his term of office, and within the limits of his jurisdiction, shall have precedence before the Sheriff Principal having concurrent jurisdiction in the said County or County of a City.

The Lord Chancellor of Great Britain.

The Moderator of the General Assembly of the Church of Scotland during his term of office.

Order of Precedency

The Prime Minister.

The Keeper of the Great Seal of Scotland (The Secretary for Scotland) (if a Peer).

The Speaker of the House of Commons.

The Keeper of the Privy Seal of Scotland (if a Peer).

The Hereditary High Constable of Scotland.

The Hereditary Master of the Household in Scotland.

Dukes of England.

Dukes of Scotland.

Dukes of Great Britain.

Dukes of United Kingdom and Dukes of Ireland created since 1801.

Eldest Sons of Dukes of Blood Royal.

Marquesses of England.

Marquesses of Scotland.

Marquesses of Great Britain.

Marquesses of the United Kingdom and Marquesses of Ireland created since the Union of Great Britain and Ireland.

Eldest Sons of Dukes.

Earls of England.

Earls of Scotland.

Earls of Great Britain.

Earls of United Kingdom and Earls of Ireland created since 1801.

Younger Sons of Dukes of Blood Royal.

Eldest Sons of Marquesses.

Younger Sons of Dukes.

The Keeper of the Great Seal (The Secretary for Scotland) (if not a Peer).

The Keeper of the Privy Seal (if not a Peer).

The Lord Justice-General.

The Lord Clerk Register.

The Lord Advocate.

The Lord Justice-Clerk.

Viscounts of England.

Viscounts of Scotland.

Viscounts of Great Britain.

Viscounts of the United Kingdom and Viscounts of Ireland created since the Union of Great Britain and Ireland.

Eldest Sons of Earls.

Younger Sons of Marquesses.

Barons of England.

Barons of Scotland

Barons of Great Britain.

Barons of United Kingdom and Barons of Ireland created since 1801.
Eldest Sons of Viscounts.
Younger Sons of Earls.
Eldest Sons of Barons.
Knights of the Garter.
Privy Councillors.
Senators of the College of Justice and Chairman of the Land Court.
Younger Sons of Viscounts.
Younger Sons of Barons.
Sons of Law Life Peers.
Baronets.
Knights of the Thistle.
Knights of St Patrick.
Knights Grand Cross of the Order of the Bath.
Knights Grand Commanders of the Order of the Star of India.
Knights Grand Cross of the Order of St Michael and St George.
Knights Grand Commanders of the Order of the Indian Empire.
Knights Grand Cross of the Royal Victorian Order.
Knights Grand Cross of the Order of the British Empire.
Knights Commanders of the Order of the Bath.
Knights Commanders of the Order of the Star of India.
Knights Commanders of the Order of St Michael and St George.
Knights Commanders of the Order of the Indian Empire.
Knights Commanders of the Royal Victorian Order.
Knights Commanders of the Order of the British Empire.
Solicitor-General for Scotland.
Lyon King of Arms.
Sheriffs Principal.
Knights Bachelor.
Sheriffs-Substitute.
Companions of the Order of the Bath.
Companions of the Order of the Star of India.
Companions of the Order of St Michael and St George.
Companions of the Order of the Indian Empire.
Commanders of the Royal Victorian Order.
Commanders of the Order of the British Empire.
Companions of the Distinguished Service Order.
Members of the Fourth Class of the Royal Victorian Order.
Officers of the Order of the British Empire.
Imperial Service Order.
Eldest Sons of Younger Sons of Peers.
Eldest Sons of Baronets.

Order of Precedency

Eldest Sons of Knights.
Members of the Fifth Class of the Royal Victorian Order.
Members of the Order of the British Empire.
Younger Sons of Baronets.
Younger Sons of Knights.
King's Counsel.
Esquires.
Gentlemen.

THE SCALE OF PRECEDENCE FOR LADIES IN SCOTLAND

The QUEEN.
The QUEEN DOWAGER.

Duchess of Rothesay.
Daughters of the Sovereign.
Wives of Younger Sons of the Sovereign.
Granddaughters of the Sovereign.
Wives of Grandsons of the Sovereign.
Sisters of the Sovereign.
Wives of Brothers of the Sovereign.
Aunts of the Sovereign.
Wives of Uncles of the Sovereign.
Nieces of the Sovereign.
Wives of Nephews of the Sovereign.
Duchesses in the rank of their Husbands, viz. :—
> Duchesses of England.
> Duchesses of Scotland.
> Duchesses of Great Britain.
> Duchesses of the United Kingdom and Duchesses of Ireland of titles created since the Union of Great Britain and Ireland.

Wives of the Eldest Sons of Dukes of Blood Royal.
Marchionesses in the rank of their Husbands, viz. :—
> Marchionesses of England.
> Marchionesses of Scotland.
> Marchionesses of Great Britain.
> Marchionesses of the United Kingdom and Marchionesses of Ireland of titles created since the Union of Great Britain and Ireland.

Wives of Eldest Sons of Dukes.
Daughters of Dukes.

Countesses in the rank of their Husbands, viz. :—

    Countesses of England.

    Countesses of Scotland.

    Countesses of Great Britain.

    Countesses of the United Kingdom and Countesses of Ireland of titles created since the Union of Great Britain and Ireland.

Wives of Younger Sons of Dukes of Blood Royal.

Wives of Eldest Sons of Marquesses.

Daughters of Marquesses.

Wives of Younger Sons of Dukes.

Viscountesses in the rank of their Husbands, viz. :—

    Viscountesses of England.

    Viscountesses of Scotland.

    Viscountesses of Great Britain.

    Viscountesses of the United Kingdom and Viscountesses of Ireland of titles created since 1801.

Wives of Eldest Sons of Earls.

Daughters of Earls.

Wives of Younger Sons of Marquesses.

Baronesses in the rank of their Husbands, viz. :—

    Baronesses of England.

    Baronesses of Scotland.

    Baronesses of Great Britain.

    Baronesses of the United Kingdom and Baronesses of Ireland of titles created since the Union of Great Britain and Ireland.

Wives of Eldest Sons of Viscounts.

Daughters of Viscounts.

Wives of Younger Sons of Earls.

Wives of Eldest Sons of Barons.

Daughters of Barons.

Maids of Honour to the Queen.

Wives of Knights of the Garter.

Wives of Younger Sons of Viscounts.

Wives of Younger Sons of Barons.

Daughters of Law Life Peers (Lords of Appeal in Ordinary).

Wives of Sons of Law Life Peers (Lords of Appeal in Ordinary).

Wives of Baronets.

Wives of Knights of the Thistle.

Wives of Knights of St Patrick.

Dames Grand Cross of the Order of the British Empire.

Wives of Knights Grand Cross of the Order of the Bath.

Wives of Knights Grand Commanders of the Order of the Star of India.

Order of Precedency

Wives of Knights Grand Cross of the Order of St Michael and St George.

Wives of Knights Grand Commanders of the Order of the Indian Empire.

Wives of Knights Grand Cross of the Royal Victorian Order.

Wives of Knights Grand Cross of the Order of the British Empire.

Dame Commanders of the Order of the British Empire.

Wives of Knights Commanders of the Order of the Bath.

Wives of Knights Commanders of the Order of the Star of India.

Wives of Knights Commanders of the Order of St Michael and St George.

Wives of Knights Commanders of the Order of the Indian Empire.

Wives of Knights Commanders of the Royal Victorian Order.

Wives of Knights Commanders of the Order of the British Empire.

Wives of Knights Bachelor and Wives of Senators of the College of Justice (Lords of Session), and of the Chairman of the Land Court.*
Taking precedence among themselves according to the dates of their husbands' creation as Knights or appointment as Senators of the College of Justice respectively.

Commanders of the Order of the British Empire.

Wives of Companions of the Order of the Bath.

Wives of Companions of the Order of the Star of India.

Wives of Companions of the Order of St Michael and St George.

Wives of Companions of the Order of the Indian Empire.

Wives of Commanders of the Royal Victorian Order.

Wives of Commanders of the Order of the British Empire.

Wives of Companions of the Distinguished Service Order.

Officers of the Order of the British Empire.

Wives of Members of the 4th Class of the Royal Victorian Order.

Wives of Eldest Sons of Younger Sons of Peers.

Daughters of Younger Sons of Peers.

Wives of Eldest Sons of Baronets.

Daughters of Baronets.

Wives of Eldest Sons of Knights of the Garter, of the Thistle, and of St Patrick.

Wives of Eldest Sons of Knights.

Daughters of Knights.

Members of the Order of the British Empire.

Wives of Members of the 5th Class of the Royal Victorian Order.

Wives of Members of the Order of the British Empire.

Members of Imperial Service Order.

Wives of Members of the Imperial Service Order.

---

* Royal warrant of 16th April 1912.

Wives of Younger Sons of Baronets.
Wives of Younger Sons of Knights.
Wives of Esquires.
Wives of Gentlemen.

The foregoing tables may in certain circumstances be departed from—*e.g.*, at a public function given in honour of a certain person, that person will take precedence of all others next the host.

Dowager peeresses take precedence of the wives of their sons.

A peeress in her own rank, or a peer's daughter who may have married a commoner, retain their own rank and status.

Baronets of the three countries or of the United Kingdom rank according to their respective creations.

Ambassadors rank after the children of the sovereign to whose court they are accredited.

Officers of the navy and army rank *inter se* according to their respective ranks.

Public bodies have no scale of precedence as between themselves, but they may have such among their own members.

There are also separate rolls of precedence for Ireland, India, and for certain of the principal Colonies.

Dictionary of Heraldic Terms

ABAISSÉ. A French word, generally used in heraldry instead of the English word abased. When the fess, or any other ordinary properly placed above the fess point of the shield, is brought below it, that ordinary is said to be *abaissé*.

ABATEMENT. Any figure added to coats of arms tending to lower the dignity or station of the bearer. Thus, the baton sinister, denoting illegitimacy, is an abatement.

ACHIEVEMENT. The coat of arms (helmet, crest, mantling, motto) fully emblazoned according to the rules of heraldry. The lozenge-shaped achievements that are displayed on the outside of the houses of persons deceased are commonly called hatchments.

ADDORSED. Any animals set back to back. See LION.

AFFRONTÉE. Showing full face or front.

ALLERION. An eagle displayed, without beak or feet.

Ex. Argent, an allerion gules.

ALTERNATE. Figures or tinctures that succeed each other by turns.

AMBULANT. In the act of walking.

Manual of Heraldry

AMETHYST.   A precious stone of a violet colour, the name
of which was formerly used instead of purpure, to
denote the purple tincture when emblazoning the arms
of the English nobility.

ANNULET.   A small circle borne as a charge
in coats of arms.

> *Ex.*   Azure, an annulet argent.   Annu-
> lets are added to arms for a dif-
> ference.   See DIFFERENCES, p. 24.

ANCIENT.   A small flag or ensign.   The bearer of the flag
was called by its name.   *Iago* was ancient to the troops
commanded by *Othello.*

> " This is Othello's ancient, as I take it.
> The same indeed, a very valiant fellow."—SHAKSPEARE.

APAUMY.   An open hand, showing the palm.

ARCHBISHOPS.   Church dignitaries of the first class.   There
are but two in England—the Archbishop of Canterbury and the Archbishop of York.   The former is the
first peer of England next to the royal family, and
has the title of *Grace* given to him; and likewise *Most
Reverend Father in God.*   He is styled *Lord Primate
of all England,* and *Metropolitan.*

The Archbishop of York has precedence of dukes
and great officers of state, except the Lord Chancellor.
He is called *His Grace* and *Most Reverend Father in
God;* and styled *Primate of England,* and *Metropolitan.*

ARGENT.   The French word for silver, of
which metal all white fields or charges
are supposed to consist.   See p. 17.

Dictionary of Heraldic Terms

ARMED. This word is used to express the horns, hoofs, beak, teeth, or talons of any beast or bird of prey, when borne of a different tincture from those of their bodies.

Ex. Crest, a demi-griffin argent, armed gules.

ARMES PARLANTES, or Canting Arms, are such as are adapted from the name of the person who bears them, *e.g.*, Bells for Bell.

ARMS. A word derived from the Latin *arma*, which signifies in heraldry a mark of honour, serving to distinguish states, cities, families, etc.

ARROWS. Short darts feathered at the ends.

Ex. Argent, three arrows paleways, points in chief sable, feathered proper.

ASPECTANT. Animals placed face to face in a charge are said to be aspectant. If they are about to attack each other, they are said to be combatant.

ASSUMPTIVE. Arms assumed without legal authority.

ASSURGENT. A man or beast rising out of the sea is said to be assurgent.

AT GAZE. See GAZE.

ATTIRED. When the horns of a stag are of a different tincture to its head, it is said to be attired of that tincture.

Ex. Argent, a stag lodged, proper, attired or.

AUGMENTATION. This word signifies in heraldry a particular mark of honour, granted by the sovereign in

Manual of Heraldry

consideration of some noble action, or by favour, and either quartered with the family arms, or borne on an escutcheon, chief, or canton.

> *Ex.* Ermine, on a chevron azure, three foxes' heads erased, argent. The augmentation is on a canton azure, a fleur-de-lis argent.

AZURE. The French word for *blue:* it is represented in heraldic engraving by parallel lines, as in the annexed example.

BADGE. A distinctive mark, without motto or wreath, worn by servants, retainers, and followers of royalty or nobility, who, being beneath the rank of gentlemen, have no right to armorial bearings. The rose and crown is the badge of the servants, etc., of the kings of England: they are displayed as in the annexed example.

BANDED. Anything tied with a band.

> *Ex.* Argent. Three arrows proper, banded gules.

BANNER. The principal flag of a knight. The great banner borne at the funeral of a nobleman contains all the quarterings of his arms: it varies in size according to the rank of the deceased. The banner of the

Dictionary of Heraldic Terms

sovereign is five feet square; that of a prince or duke, four feet square; for all noblemen of inferior rank, three feet square.

BANNER ROLL is a small square flag containing a single escutcheon of the deceased. Thus, if there are twelve quarterings in the banner, the same number of banner rolls will be required to be borne in the funeral procession. The annexed engraving shows the banner and banner roll.

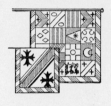

BAR. A diminutive of the fess (*q.v.*), occupying one-fifth of the shield. It may be placed in any part of the field. It has two diminutives, the closet and barulet.

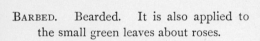

Ex. Ermine, two bars gules.

BARBED. Bearded. It is also applied to the small green leaves about roses.

Ex. Azure, a rose argent, barbed, and seeded proper.

BARDINGS. Horse trappings charged with armorial bearings.

BARON. The lowest title of the peerage of Great Britain. It originally was a dignity held in conjunction with the possession of certain lands held under feudal tenure, on condition of performing certain services to the king. In the reign of King John the right to sit in Parliament was restricted to those barons who should be specially summoned by royal writ. The creation of peers by writ of summons was, however, superseded in the time of Richard II. by the introduction of letters patent. The first person ennobled in this manner was John Beauchamp of Holt, who was created Baron Beauchamp by letters patent dated 10th October 1387. This form of creating lords of parliament was introduced into Scotland by James I., and a distinction made between the minor barons (or landed proprietors who held their estates under a charter of barony) and these lords. A baron's mantle has two rows of ermine, and his coronet, a circlet of silver gilt, surmounted by six silver balls at equal distances, with cap of crimson velvet having a golden tassel on the top, was first granted by King Charles II.

BARON AND FEMME. Terms used in heraldry to denote the arms of a man and his wife, marshalled together. See pp. 35-38.

BARONET. See KNIGHT BARONET.

BARRULET. The smallest diminutive of the bar. The closet is half the bar : the barrulet half the closet.

Ex. Gules, two barrulets argent.

BARRY. A field divided transversely into several equal parts exceeding five in number, and consisting of two different tinctures interchangeably disposed. They must always be an even number.

Ex. Barry of eight pieces, azure and argent.

Dictionary of Heraldic Terms

BARS, GEMELS. See GEMELS.

BAR-WISE. Crossing the field in the manner of a bar.

BASE. The lowest part of the shield.

BATON. BATUNE. BASTON. Is a fourth part of the bend, and is couped at both ends. It is generally used in England as an abatement in coats of arms to denote illegitimacy, and is seldom used except by the natural issue of royalty and their descendants, and is then represented as a baton sinister.

> *Ex.* Or, a cross gules, over all a baton sinister argent.

BATTERING RAM. An instrument used for battering down walls previous to the use of gunpowder.

> *Ex.* Argent, a battering ram proper.

BATTLE AXE. An ancient military weapon.

> *Ex.* Argent, three battle axes gules, two over one.

BEAKED. The beak of a bird being of a different tint from the body is said to be beaked of a tincture or metal.

> *Ex.* An eagle's head erased gules, beaked or.

Manual of Heraldry

BEAVER. That part of the helmet that defends the sight.

BELLED. Having bells.

Ex. Argent, a barrulet gules, belled with three bells proper.

BEND. One of the honourable ordinaries formed by two diagonal lines drawn from the dexter chief to the sinister base; it generally occupies a fifth part of the shield if uncharged, but if charged, one-third.

Ex. Azure, a bend argent.

BEND SINISTER. Is the reverse of the bend, being drawn from the sinister to the dexter side of the shield; it is seldom found in coats of arms, as it is reckoned an abatement.

Ex. Argent, a bend sinister gules.

IN BEND. Figures placed in a slanting direction from the dexter chief to the sinister base are said to be in bend.

Ex. Or, three torteaux in bend.

Dictionary of Heraldic Terms

BENDLET. A diminutive of the bend, of the same shape, but only half the width of the bend.

> *Ex.* Gules, two bendlets invected argent.

BENDY. This word serves to denote a field divided diagonally into several bends, varying in metal and colour.

> *Ex.* Bendy of six pieces, azure and argent.

BESANT, or BEZANT. Gold coin of Byzantium; when they appear in a coat of arms their colour is not described : a besant is always or.

BEVILLY. Dovetailed.

BILLETS. This charge is, by some authors, supposed to represent tiles or bricks; by others that it represents a letter or billet. The name and form of the charge most accords with the latter opinion.

> *Ex.* Argent, three billets azure, two over one.

BISHOPS of the Church of England are spiritual peers of the realm, and as such have precedence next to viscounts, the Bishops of London, Durham, and Winchester preceding the others, who rank according to date of appointment. Twenty-four of their number sit in the House of Lords.

Manual of Heraldry

BLAZON. To describe in proper heraldic language and colours all that belongs to coats of arms.

BORDURE, or BORDER. This is the most ancient difference in coats of arms, to distinguish different branches of the same family. It is a border round the edge of the shield. Its situation is always the same; but the inner edge may be varied.

> *Ex.* Argent, a sinister hand couped at the wrist and erected gules, within a bordure azure.

BOTTONNY. See CROSS BOTTONNY.

BOUGET. An ancient water-bucket, frequently borne in shields of arms.

> *Ex.* Argent, a bouget proper.

BRACED. Two figures of the same form, interlacing each other.

> *Ex.* Vert, two triangles braced, argent.

BRASED and BRAZED are words sometimes used by ancient armorists. They always describe things interlaced or braced together.

BRISURE. A mark of cadency or difference.

Dictionary of Heraldic Terms

BROAD ARROW. An ancient weapon of war, thrown by an engine. It is frequently borne as a charge in coats of arms.

Ex. Argent, a broad arrow gules.

BROUCHANT. Placed over, or overlying.

CABOCHED, CABOSHED, or CABOSSED. Beasts' heads borne without any part of the neck, and full faced.

Ex. Argent, a stag's head caboshed, proper.

CADENCY. See p. 23.

CALTRAP, or CHEVAL TRAP. An iron instrument made to annoy an enemy's cavalry. They were formed of iron, being four spikes conjoined in such a manner that one was always upwards. It is found in many ancient coats of arms.

Ex. Argent, a caltrap proper.

CANTING HERALDRY. See ARMES PARLANTES.

CANTON. The French word for corner. It is a small square figure, generally placed at the dexter chief of the shield, as in the annexed example. When it is charged the size may be increased. It is said to represent the banner of the ancient knights banneret.

Manual of Heraldry

CELESTIAL CROWN. Distinguished from any
other crown by the stars on the points
or rays that proceed from the circlet.

CHAMPAGNE. A narrow piece cut off the base of a shield
by a straight line.

CHAPEAU. Cap of maintenance or dignity, borne only by
sovereign princes. It is formed of
crimson or scarlet velvet, lined with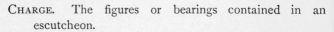
ermine. In certain crests it is used in place of the
torse or crest wreath.

CHAPLET. An ancient ornament for the head, granted to
gallant knights for acts of courtesy. It is frequently
borne as a charge in a shield of arms,
and always tinted in its natural colours.

Ex. Argent, a chaplet proper.

CHARGE. The figures or bearings contained in an
escutcheon.

CHECKY. The field covered with alternate
squares of metal or colour and fur.

Ex. Checky, sable and argent.

CHEVRON. This ordinary is supposed to
represent the rafters of the gable of a
house.

Ex. Or a chevron gules.

Dictionary of Heraldic Terms

CHEVRON COUCHED. One which springs from either the dexter or sinister side of the shield.

CHEVRONEL. The diminutive of the chevron, being one-half its size.

Ex. Argent, two chevronels gules.

CHIEF. One of the honourable ordinaries. It is placed on the upper part of the shield and contains a third part of it. The letters show the points in the chief. A is the dexter chief; B, the middle chief; C, the sinister chief.

CHIMERICAL FIGURES. Imaginary figures, such as griffins, dragons, harpies, etc.; all of them will be found under their proper names.

CINQUE FOIL. Five leaves conjoined in the centre.

CIVIC CAP. A cap of dignity borne by mayors of cities or corporate bodies: it is formed of sables garnished with ermine.

CIVIC CROWN. A wreath of oak leaves and acorns.

CLARION. This charge is so called from its resemblance to a horn or trumpet. It is really a lance rest.

Ex. Azure, three clarions or.

Manual of Heraldry

CLENCHED. The fingers pressed towards the palm of the hand.

> *Ex.* Azure, a dexter arm vambraced couped, the fist clenched proper.

CLOSE. Applied to a bird with its wings closed.

CLOSET. A diminutive of the bar, being only one-half its width.

> *Ex.* Or, two closets azure.

CLOSEGIRT. A figure whose dress is fastened round the waist.

> *Ex.* Gules, an angel erect with wings expanded or, dress closegirt.

CLOUÉ. Nailed, said of horseshoes, etc., when the nails are of a different tincture.

COAT ARMOUR, or SURCOAT. A loose garment worn over the armour of a knight; hence the term coat of arms. On this garment were emblazoned the armorial bearings of the wearer.

Dictionary of Heraldic Terms

COCKADE. The black cockade is worn by the servants of persons holding direct commission from the sovereign, and dates from the time of George I., who bore it as a vassal of the Emperor. There are two varieties—the fan-shaped, which is the military, and a round shape, which is naval and civil.

COCKATRICE. A chimerical animal, a cock with a dragon's tail and wings and two legs.

COLLARED. Having a collar. Dogs and inferior animals are sometimes collared; the supporters and charges are generally said to be gorged. See GORGED.

COMBATANT. A French word for fighting. See LION.

COMPARTMENT. A panel or mound placed below the shield on which the supporters rest; or occasionally a motto may be placed.

COMPLEMENT. The heraldic term for the full moon. When this figure is introduced as a charge in a coat of arms, it is called a moon in her complement.

COMPONY. A term applied to a bordure, pale, bend, or any other ordinary, made up of squares of alternate metal and colour. The bordure compony is the mark of illegitimacy in Scotland.

Ex. Argent, an inescutcheon azure, a bordure compony or and gules.

Manual of Heraldry

CONJOINED. Joined together.

> *Ex.* Argent, three legs armed, conjoined at the fess point at the upper extremity of the thigh, flexed in a triangle, garnished and spurred or.

CONTOURNÉE. Facing the sinister.

CONY. An heraldic name for a young rabbit.

CORDON. A silver cord which encircles the arms of a widow.

CORONET. See CROWN.

COTISE. One of the diminutives of the bend, being one-fourth of its size; cotises are generally borne on each side of the bend.

> *Ex.* Gules, a bend argent, between two cotises of the same.

The cotises are frequently of a different tincture from the bend they cotise.

COUCHANT. The French word for lying down with the breast towards the earth, and the head raised. See LION COUCHANT.

COUCHÉE. Is applied to a shield when it is placed in a diagonal position.

COUNT. A nobleman that was deputed by the king to govern a county or shire: the title is not used in the British Peerage; his rank is equal to an earl.

Dictionary of Heraldic Terms

COUNTER. In heraldry implies contrariety, as in the following examples:—

COUNTER-CHANGED. Is the division of the shield into two parts, one colour and one metal, and arranging that the charges placed upon the metal are of the colour, and *vice versa*.

> *Ex.* Per pale, or and azure, on a chevron, three mullets all counter-changed.

COUNTER-COMPONY. Is applied to an ordinary of two checks in width of alternating tinctures.

COUNTER-EMBATTLED. Embattled on both sides.

COUNTER-FLORY. Any ordinary ornamented with fleurs-de-luce: the points of the flowers run alternately in a contrary direction.

> *Ex.* Or, a pale purpure, flory and counter-flory gules.

COUNTER-PASSANT. Two animals passing the contrary way to each other.

> *Ex.* Or, two lions passant counter-passant gules, the uppermost facing the sinister side of the escutcheon, both collared sable, garnished argent.

COUNTER-SALIENT. Two animals leaping different ways from each other.

> *Ex.* Argent, two foxes counter-salient proper.

Manual of Heraldry

COUPED. From the French word *couper*, to cut. The cross in the example is coupled, part of it being cut off, so as not to touch the edges of the shield.

Ex. Azure, a cross couped argent.

COUPED. The head or limbs of any animal cut close is called couped.

Ex. Argent, a boar's head couped proper.

COUPLE-CLOSE. One of the diminutives of the chevron, half the size of the chevronel.

Ex. Argent, three couple-closes inter-laced vert.

COURANT. Running.

Ex. Argent, a stag courant proper.

COWARD, or COUÉ. Signifies an animal with its tail between its legs.

CRENELLE. The French heraldic term for embattled. See EMBATTLED.

Dictionary of Heraldic Terms

CRESCENT. The crescent moon with its horns turned upwards.

Ex. Azure, a crescent argent.

CREST. The ornament on the upper part of the helmet in heraldry placed over coats of arms.

The English royal crest is a crown surmounted by a lion statant guardant crowned, or.

The Scottish royal crest is an imperial crown surmounted by a lion sejant guardant, displaying a sceptre and sword or.

The Irish royal crest is an ancient diadem surmounted by an embattled tower, a stag courant issuing from the portal.

The crest of Wales is a dragon passant guardant, gules.

Crests are usually displayed upon a wreath as in the annexed example, which is a demi-lion rampant; but when they issue from a crown, coronet, or cap of maintenance they have no wreath. Ladies, with the exception of the sovereign, have no crest. See HELMET, WREATH, and MANTLING.

CRESTED. A cock or other bird, whose comb is of a different tincture from the body, is said to be crested.

Manual of Heraldry

CRINED. This is said of an animal whose hair is of a different tincture from its body.

Ex. Argent, a mermaid gules, crined or.

CROSIER. The pastoral staff of a bishop or abbot: a very frequent charge in ecclesiastical arms.

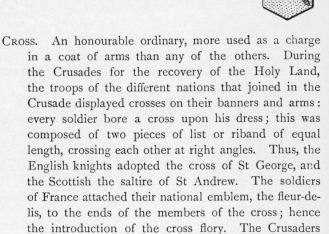

Ex. Or, a crosier gules, in bend.

CROSS. An honourable ordinary, more used as a charge in a coat of arms than any of the others. During the Crusades for the recovery of the Holy Land, the troops of the different nations that joined in the Crusade displayed crosses on their banners and arms: every soldier bore a cross upon his dress; this was composed of two pieces of list or riband of equal length, crossing each other at right angles. Thus, the English knights adopted the cross of St George, and the Scottish the saltire of St Andrew. The soldiers of France attached their national emblem, the fleur-de-lis, to the ends of the members of the cross; hence the introduction of the cross flory. The Crusaders from the Papal dominions placed transverse pieces on each member of the plain cross, and by this means transformed it into four small crosses springing from a centre, forming what is now called the cross crosslet. It would be impossible within the limits of this work to give an example of all the crosses that have been introduced as bearings in coats of arms. Berry, in his

Dictionary of Heraldic Terms

comprehensive work on heraldry, gives nearly two hundred examples, without giving all that might be found. The following are the crosses most used in British heraldry.

Cross.

Cross potent.

Cross flory.

Cross crosslet.

Cross bottonny.

Cross pattee.

Cross raguly.

Cross patonce.

Manual of Heraldry

Cross moline.

Cross quadrate.

Cross quarter-pierced.

Cross of Calvary.

Cross fitchy.

Cross patriarchal.

Cross potent
rebated.

CROWN AND CORONETS.

The crown of the King of
the United Kingdom.

Coronet of the Prince
of Wales.

Of a royal duke.

Of a princess of Britain.

Dictionary of Heraldic Terms

Of a duke.

Of a marquess.

Of an earl.

Of a viscount.

Coronet of a baron

CRUSILY. Having the field semée of crosses crosslet.

CUBIT ARM. The hand and arm cut off at the elbow.

CURTANA. The pointless sword of mercy is the principal in dignity of the three swords that are borne naked before the British monarchs at their coronation.

DANCETTÉ. A zig-zag figure with spaces between the points, much larger than in the indented.

Ex. Argent, a pale, dancetté vert.

DEBRUISED. Any charge that has an ordinary placed upon it is said to be debruised.

Ex. Argent, a lion rampant guard-ant gules, debruised by a fess azure.

DECRESSANT, or DECRESCENT. A moon in its wane, whose horns are turned to the sinister side of the escutcheon.

Ex. Azure, a moon decrescent proper.

DEGRADED. Applied to a cross where the arms end in steps.

DEMI, or DEMY. This particle is always joined to a substantive, and signifies half; as, a demi-lion, *i.e.*, half a lion.

DETRIMENT. The moon is said to be in its detriment when it is eclipsed.

Ex. Argent, the moon in her detriment sable.

DEXTER. A word used in heraldry to signify the proper right side of anything; that is, the side on the left of the spectator.

DIADEM. A circle of gold with points rising from it, worn by ancient kings as the token of royalty. The diadem of most of the monarchs of Europe, as represented in ancient statuary, stained glass and paintings, resembles the annexed engraving; the kings of England, from the Conquest to Henry VII., all wore a diadem of this shape.

DIAMOND. The hardest and most valuable of precious stones; it was formerly used by English heralds to denote black or sable in blazoning the arms of the nobility.

Dictionary of Heraldic Terms

DIFFERENCE. The term given to a certain figure added to coats of arms to distinguish one family from another, and to show how distant younger branches are from the elder or principal branch. See p. 23.

DIMIDIATED. Is when two coats in union are divided per pale, and one half of each removed.

DIMINUTION. A word sometimes used instead of difference.

DISMEMBERED or Couped in all the points. Cut in pieces, but without any alteration in the form of the original figure.

DISPLAYED. A bird whose wings are expanded and legs spread is said to be displayed.

Ex. Argent, an eagle displayed sable.

DISTINGUISHED SERVICE ORDER. Instituted 6th September 1886, is conferred on officers of the navy and army who have been honourably mentioned in despatches of meritorious or distinguished service in war.

DORMANT. The French word for sleeping, used to denote the posture of a lion, or any other beast reposing. See LION.

DOUBLINGS. The lining of robes of state, and also of the mantlings in coats of arms.

DOUBLE TRESSURE. Two tressures, or orles, one within the other.

Manual of Heraldry

DOUBLE TRESSURE FLORY COUNTER-FLORY
which surrounds the Royal Arms of
Scotland is not now granted in Scotland
to subjects except as a mark of royal
favour. It is generally indicative of
royal descent.

DOVETAILED. A term borrowed from carpentry to show
tinctures joined together by reversed wedges, which,
being shaped like doves' tails, are by joiners called
dovetailing.

> *Ex.* Quarterly per pale dovetailed, or
> and gules.

DRAGON. An imaginary monster with four legs; a mix-
ture of beast, bird, and reptile. It is frequently borne
in crests and charges.

> *Ex.* Argent, a dragon proper, tail
> nowed vert.

DRAGON'S HEAD. Part of a celestial constellation, used
by ancient English heralds to denote tenné when emblazoning the arms of sovereigns; this style of heraldry
has become obsolete.

DRAGON'S TAIL. Part of the same constellation; formerly
used to denote sanguine.

DUKE. The highest degree of British peerage next to the
Prince of Wales. This title is derived from the Latin
word *dux :* the title of duke was known in other parts

Dictionary of Heraldic Terms

of Europe long before it was introduced into England. The first person that was created a duke in that country was Edward the Black Prince, who was created Duke of Cornwall in 1337 by his father, Edward III. The title has since that time belonged to the first-born son of the monarch of England. The earliest dukedom in Scotland was that of Rothesay, bestowed in 1398 by King Robert III. on his eldest son, a title still borne by the Prince of Wales, and at the same time the King's brother, the Earl of Fife, was advanced to the dignity of Duke of Albany. His mantle has four rows of ermine on the cape, and his coronet is formed of a circle of gold, surmounted by eight golden strawberry leaves, with a cap of crimson velvet, turned up ermine, and surmounted by a golden tassel (see p. 75).

EAGLE. *Aquila* in ornithology. In heraldry the eagle is accounted one of the most noble bearings. It is sometimes borne double headed as in the arms of the Emperor.

EAGLET is a diminutive of eagle, properly signifying a young eagle. In heraldry, when several eagles are on the same escutcheon, they are termed eaglets.

EARL. The third degree of British peerage. Under the Danish and Saxon kings this was the highest title known in England conferred upon a subject. The dignity both in England and Scotland originally was territorial, and a part and pertinent of the lands comprised in the earldom and the title passed with the ownership of the estate. For many centuries earldoms have been created by Letters Patent under the Great Seal, the succession being in terms of the remainder contained therein. An earl's mantle has three rows of ermine on the cape, and his coronet is a circle of silver gilt surmounted by eight silver balls raised on points with gold strawberry leaves between the points, and a cap of crimson velvet, turned up ermine, and surmounted with a golden tassel.

EARL MARSHAL OF ENGLAND. A very ancient, and formerly a very important, officer, who had several courts under his jurisdiction, as the Court of Chivalry, the Court of Honour. He still presides over the Heralds' College, and nominally over the Marshalsea Court. The title of Earl Marshal of England is now, and has been for some centuries, hereditary in the family of Howard, Duke of Norfolk. He has no jurisdiction out of England. The Earl Marischal of Scotland, a title held by the Keith family, and attainted in the person of George, 10th Earl, in 1716, had no jurisdiction in matters armorial.

EASTERN or ANTIQUE CROWN. A crown with rays proceeding from a circle, called by heralds an Eastern crown, is found in ancient achievements. The annexed cut shows its form.

ELEVATED. Applied to wings raised above the head.

EMBATTLED. A line, formed like the battlements on a wall or tower, is said to be embattled or crenelle. When the line is used to form one of the ordinaries, that ordinary is said to be embattled. See the lines, p. 21.

Ex. Gules, three towers embattled argent.

Dictionary of Heraldic Terms

When a fess, chevron, or bend is said to be embattled it is only so on the upper side, but when embattled on both sides it is called counter-embattled.

Ex. Gules, a bend sinister embattled argent.

EMBATTLED GRADY. Where the embattlements gradually rise one above another.

Ex. Argent, a fess gules, embattled grady. See the lines, p. 22.

EMBOWED. Anything bent or curved, like a bow.

Ex. Gules, a dolphin naiant embowed or.

EMERALD. The name of a precious stone formerly substituted for vert in emblazoning the arms of the nobility of England.

EN ARRIÈRE. An expression borrowed from the French, to signify any creature borne with its back to view.

Ex. Argent, an eagle proper en arrière.

Manual of Heraldry

ENDORSE. The smallest diminutive of the pale, being one-fourth of its size. It is never charged with anything.

> *Ex.* Argent, a pale between endorses gules.

ENFILED. Applies to a weapon which pierces or passes through another object, such as a heart, a ring, etc.

ENGRAILED. Any object being edged with small semicircles, the points turning outwards, is said to be engrailed.

> *Ex.* Argent, a pale azure engrailed.

ENHANCED. A term applied to bearings placed above their usual situation.

> *Ex.* Argent, three bendlets, enhanced gules.

ENSIGNED. This word, in heraldic description, means having some charge placed above.

> *Ex.* Argent, a man's heart gules, ensigned with a celestial crown or.

ENTIRE. Means that the charge is extended to the side of the shield.

ERADICATED. Torn up by the roots.

Dictionary of Heraldic Terms

ERASED. Signifies anything torn or plucked off, with a ragged edge, from the part to which nature affixed it ; generally applied to the head and limbs of man or beast.

> *Ex.* Argent, a leg erased at the midst of the thigh gules.

ERECT. This is said of any charge, naturally horizontal, being placed in a perpendicular direction.

> *Ex.* Argent, a boar's head erect, and erased.

ERMINE. A white fur with black spots, represented as in the annexed example. See p. 19.

ERMINES. This fur is represented by white spots on a black field. See p. 19.

ERMINOIS. A fur, the field or, the spots or tufts sable, as in the annexed example. See p. 19.

ESCALLOP. The shell of a sea-fish, used to decorate the palmers on their way to and from Palestine; frequently used as a charge in heraldry.

ESCARBUNCLE. A charge originally formed from the iron bands radiating from the centre of the shield to strengthen it.

ESCROLL. The roll or strip of parchment on which the motto is placed.

ESCUTCHEON. This word is sometimes used to express the whole coat of arms, sometimes only the field upon which the arms are painted.
It more generally denotes the painted shields used at funerals. The field, if the husband is dead and wife survives, is black on the dexter side only; if the wife is deceased, it is black on the sinister side; if both, it is black all over. The example shows that this is the escutcheon of a deceased baron, whose lady survives. See p. 38

ESCUTCHEON OF PRETENCE. A small escutcheon, on which a man bears the coat of arms of his wife, who is an heiress. See p. 36.

> *Ex.* Argent, a chevron or, between three crosslets sable, on an escutcheon of pretence gules, three quatrefoils argent.

ESQUIRE. The degree below a knight and above a gentleman. Those to whom this title is due by right are

Dictionary of Heraldic Terms

all the younger sons of noblemen and their eldest sons in perpetuity, the eldest sons of baronets, of all knights and of their eldest sons in perpetuity, kings of arms, heralds, officers of the navy and army of rank of captain and upwards, sheriffs of counties for life, J.P.'s, serjeants-at-law, king's counsel, serjeants-at-arms, companions of orders of knighthood, certain officers of royal household, deputy lieutenants, commissioners of the court of bankruptcy, masters of the supreme court, royal academicians, and any person whom the sovereign designs "esquire" in a commission. For the helmet of an esquire, see p. 93.

ESTOILE. The French word for a star. It differs from the mullet in the number of points, and four of the points being rayant.

FER-DE-MOLINE. Same as Millrind (*q.v.*).

FESS. An honourable ordinary occupying the third part of the shield between the centre and the base, formed by two horizontal lines drawn above and below the centre of the shield.

Ex. Argent, a fess gules.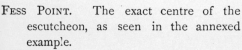

FESS POINT. The exact centre of the escutcheon, as seen in the annexed example.

FETTERLOCK. A handcuff.

Manual of Heraldry

FIELD. The whole surface of the shield or escutcheon; it is the ground upon which the tinctures, furs, ordinaries, and charges are represented.

FIGURED. Those bearings which are depicted with a human face are said to be figured.

Ex. Gules, three bezants figured proper.

FILLET. The only diminutive belonging to the chief; its width is one-fourth of the chief, and is always placed at the base of it.

FIMBRIATED. An ordinary having a narrow border of a different tincture is said to be fimbriated.

Ex. Azure, a bend gules, fimbriated argent.

FITCHY. Is from the French word *fiché*, fixed. It is generally applied to crosses which have their lower branch pointed, so that it could be fixed in the ground. See CROSS FITCHY.

FLAG. See BANNER, STANDARD, GONFANAN, GUIDON, PENNON.

FLANCHES. Are formed of two curved lines placed opposite and nearly touching each other in the centre of the shield.

Ex. Azure, a flanche argent.

Dictionary of Heraldic Terms

FLANK. The dexter and sinister sides of an escutcheon between the chief and the base.

> *Ex.* Argent, three mullets gules, accompanied with seven cross crosslets fitchy sable—three in chief, one in fess, two in flanks, one in base.

FLASQUES. A subordinate ordinary formed by curved lines placed opposite each other, but not so near as in flanches.

> *Ex.* Azure, a flasque argent.

FLEUR-DE-LIS. Supposed to represent the garden-lily. It is the bearing of the Bourbons of France, and is not an infrequent charge on British arms. It is the mark of a sixth son.

FLEXED. Bent or bowed.

FLORY. Signifies flowered or adorned with the fleur-de-lis.

FOUNTAIN. A roundel that is barry wavy of six argent and azure.

FOURCHÉE, QUEUE FOURCHÉE. Divided into two parts, *e.g.*, a lion with a double tail.

FRET. Two laths interlaced in saltire with a mascle.

> *Ex.* Azure, a fret argent.

Manual of Heraldry

FRETTY. This word denotes a field covered with fretwork or laths, crossing each other diagonally and interlacing each other.

Ex. Gules, fretty argent.

FRUCTED. Bearing fruit or seeds.

FURISONS. Representations of the steel with which a flint was struck.

THE FUSIL. Is longer and narrower than the lozenge : the upper and lower ends are more acute.

Ex. Or, a fusil purpure.

GALLEY, or LYMPHAD. An ancient vessel propelled by oars. It is largely used in the arms of those West Highland clans who formed the vassals of the ancient Lord of the Isles.

GAMB. An obsolete French word, signifying a leg, and is still used in heraldry, for the leg of a lion or other creature borne in coats of arms.

GARB. The heraldic term for a sheaf of any kind of corn.

Ex. Argent, a garb proper.

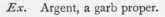

Dictionary of Heraldic Terms

GARNISHED. Ornamented.

GARTER, or BENDLET. One of the diminutives of the bend, being half the size.

Ex. Or, a garter vert.

GARTER. One of the insignia of the most noble order of the knights of the garter. It is formed of blue velvet edged with gold wire, and lined with white satin; on the velvet is embroidered the motto of the order, HONI SOIT QUI MAL Y PENSE. See KNIGHT.

GAUNTLET. Armour for the hand.

GAZE. An intent look. This is said of a deer standing still, and turning its head to look earnestly at any object.

Ex. Argent, a stag at gaze proper.

GEMELS. This word is a corruption of the French word jumelles, which signifies double. The example contains two double bars, which in heraldic language would be called two bars gemels.

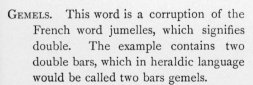

Manual of Heraldry

GILLYFLOWER. A flower resembling a carnation or pink.

GOBONY. Same as Compony (*q.v.*).

GOLPS. Roundels of a purple tincture. The colour is not stated, as the name denotes the colour.

GONFANAN. A long flag suspended from a transverse bar attached to a staff, and pointed or swallow-tailed. It is an ecclesiastical banner.

GORGED. Any animals that have collars round the neck are said to be gorged.

> *Ex.* A swan's head erased at the neck, ducally gorged or.

GORGES. Whirlpools.

GRIFFIN, or GRYPHON. A chimerical animal, the fore part having the head, legs, and talons of an eagle, and the other part, with tail and hind legs, being that of the lion. It has large wings, like an eagle's.

GUARDANT. Looking out from the field.

GUIDON. A small semi-oval flag used in funeral processions. It is generally charged with the paternal arms of the deceased.

GUIGE. A shoulder belt worn over right shoulder and used sometimes to support the shield.

GULES. Signifies red. It is represented in engraving by lines running parallel with each other, from the chief to the base, as in the example. See p. 18.

Dictionary of Heraldic Terms

GUTTÉE. A term derived from the Latin word *gutta*, a drop. A field is sprinkled or semée of drops of gold, silver, de larmes (tears), de sang (blood), etc.

GUZES. Roundels of a sanguine tincture.

GYRON. A triangular figure formed by two lines from one of the angles of the shield to the centre. The gyron may be drawn in any part of the shield, but it is generally placed as in the annexed example.

GYRONNY. When the field is covered with gyrons, their points uniting in the centre.

> *Ex.* Gyronny of eight pieces, azure, argent and gules.

HABERGEON. A coat of mail: it is also called a corselet and cuirass

> *Ex.* Argent, an habergeon proper.

HABITED. Clothed figures, either as charges or supporters, are said to be habited.

HAME. A horse collar.

HARPY. A chimerical animal, having the head and breast of a woman, and the body and legs of a bird.

Manual of Heraldry

HATCHMENT, or FUNERAL ESCUTCHEON. See p. 38.

HAURIANT. A fish, in a perpendicular direction, with its head upwards.

Ex. Argent, a salmon hauriant proper.

HELMET. An ancient piece of defensive armour for the head; it covered the face, leaving an aperture in the front, secured by bars: this was called the visor. The helmet is now placed over a coat of arms; and by the metal from which it is made, the form, and position, denotes the rank of the person whose arms are emblazoned beneath it.

The helmets of sovereigns are formed of burnished gold: those of princes and peers, of every degree, silver, garnished with gold; knights, esquires, and gentlemen, polished steel.

All helmets were placed on profile till about the year 1600, when the present arrangements appear to have been introduced into armory.

The position of the helmet is a mark of distinction. The direct front view of the grated helmet belongs to sovereign princes, and has six bars.

The grated helmet in profile is common to all degrees or peerage, with five bars.

Dictionary of Heraldic Terms

The helmet without bars, with the beaver open, standing directly fronting the spectator, denotes a baronet or knight.

The closed helmet seen in profile is appropriated to esquires and gentlemen. See CREST, BEAVER, MANTLING.

HERALD. See p. 10.

HILTED. The handle of a sword tinctured.

Ex. Argent, a sword proper couped, hilted or.

HONOUR POINT. That part of the shield between the middle chief and the fess point. In the annexed example the large dot in the centre shows the fess point; the point within the letter D, the *honour point.*

HORNED. This term is used to denote that the horn of a unicorn is of a different tincture from his body.

Ex. Azure, three unicorns' heads erased proper, horned or.

Manual of Heraldry

HUMETTY. A term used to denote an ordinary, parts of which are couped or cut off, so that it does not touch the edges of the shield.

Ex. Argent, a fess humetty gules, between three mullets sable.

HURST. A clump of trees.

HURTS. Blue roundels: the colour is expressed in the name; therefore the tincture is not otherwise named in emblazoning a coat of arms.

IMBRUED. Weapons spotted with blood are said to be imbrued. The example shows a spearhead imbrued.

IMPALED. Two coats of arms, conjoined paleways, in one shield.

Ex. Argent, a fess gules, impaled with argent, a bend azure. See p. 35.

IMPERIAL SERVICE ORDER. Instituted 8th August 1902, and conferred on civil servants after twenty-five years' (sixteen years in an unhealthy region and twenty in India) meritorious service.

INCRESCENT. The new moon, with her horns turned towards the dexter side of the shield.

Ex. Azure, a moon increscent argent.

94

Dictionary of Heraldic Terms

INDENTED.   A serrated figure, much smaller than the dancetté.

    Ex.   Or, a chief gules, indented.

INESCUTCHEON.   The name given to small escutcheons forming a bearing of a coat of arms.

    Ex.   Argent, three inescutcheons gules.

INVECTED.   A line formed with small semicircles, with the points turned inward.   Any ordinary drawn with this line is called invected.

    Ex.   Argent, a bend gules, invected between two hurts.

IRRADIATED.   Surrounded by rays of light.

ISSUANT, or ISSUING.   Proceeding from, or issuing out of.

JESSES.   Straps of hawk's bells.

KING OF ARMS.   See p. 10 *et seq.*

KNIGHT.   A title of honour conferred upon a subject for eminent services performed in war.   In the course of time, knights who had gained riches and high titles formed societies under the control and direction of their monarchs in every part of Europe.   The limits of this work will only permit us to notice the orders of knighthood introduced into Britain.

Manual of Heraldry

The KNIGHTS-BACHELORS were the earliest order of knighthood in England. The title was formerly only conferred for services in war. It was merely personal, and, like the knighthood conferred upon individuals at the present time, did not descend to their posterity.

KNIGHTS-BANNERET. This ancient and honourable order has become extinct. It obtained the title of banneret from the knights having the right of having a square banner borne before them on the field of battle, and at jousts and tournaments. Sir W. Segar gives the following account of the creation of a knight-banneret:—"It is a military order, and can only be conferred upon persons that have performed some heroic act in the field. When this action is known to the king, or general of the army, he commands the attendance of the gallant warrior, who is led, between two knights, into the presence of the king or general 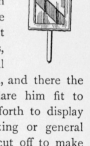 with his pennon of arms in his hand, and there the heralds proclaim his merit, and declare him fit to become a knight-banneret, and thenceforth to display a banner in the field. Then the king or general causes the point of the pennon to be cut off to make it square; it is then placed at the top of his lance, and the new-made knight returns to his tent, the trumpets sounding before him." Knights-banneret were certainly created in the reign of Edward I., but how long before that time it is impossible to tell.

KNIGHTS OF THE GARTER. This is the oldest and most honourable order of knighthood in Europe: it was founded by Edward III. in 1344; the fraternity con-

Dictionary of Heraldic Terms

sists of twenty-five knights, to which are added the princes of the blood royal. The King is the sovereign of the order; their officers are a prelate, chancellor, registrar, and king of arms.

The college of the order is in Windsor Castle, with the chapel of St George and the chapter-house. These buildings were erected by the royal founder expressly for the accommodation of the Knights of the Garter.

The garter is considered the principal ensign of this order: it is worn on the left leg below the knee; it is formed of blue velvet, edged with gold: on the velvet is embroidered the motto of the order, HONI SOIT QUI MAL Y PENSE (Dishonoured be he who thinks ill of it).

The collar is of gold, weighing thirty ounces troy weight, and contains twenty-six enamelled garters, and within each a red rose; the garters are connected by knots. Attached to this collar is a pendant representing St George (the patron Saint of the order) attacking the dragon; it is of gold enamelled, and may be enriched with jewels at the pleasure of the possessor.

KNIGHTS OF THE THISTLE. The most ancient Order of the Thistle was revived by James VII., King of Great Britain, 1687, and incorporated by Queen Anne in 1703, whose statutes were confirmed by George I. The order consists of the sovereign and sixteen brethren or knights. Their motto is NEMO ME IMPUNE LACESSIT; their badge or jewel, St Andrew, supporting a cross, surrounded with rays of gold. The officers of the order include a chancellor, dean, secretary, king of arms, and gentleman usher of the Green

Manual of Heraldry

Rod. The chapel of the order is in St Giles Cathedral, Edinburgh.

KNIGHTS OF ST PATRICK. This illustrious Irish order was founded by George III., 1783. It consists of the sovereign, a grand master, the princes of the blood royal, and twenty-two knights. The lord-lieutenant for the time being is grand master. The device on the jewel of this order is argent, a saltire gules surmounted with a trefoil vert, charged with three imperial crowns or, the whole inclosed in a circle of gold, bearing the motto QUIS SEPARABIT. MDCCLXXXIII.

KNIGHTS BARONET. A degree of honour next to a baron, created by King James VII., in 1619, to induce the English gentry to settle in the province of Ulster. The title is knight and baronet; it is hereditary. The arms of baronets of England, Great Britain, and the United Kingdom are distinguished by an augmentation of a human hand gules, borne on an escutcheon in the centre or chief of the shield.

KNIGHT BARONET OF NOVA SCOTIA. An order instituted by King James VI., in 1625, to induce capitalists to settle in that part of North America. The title is hereditary: the arms, which are borne on a canton, or on a badge suspended below the shield, are argent, St Andrew's Cross azure, surtout an escutcheon or, with a lion rampant gules within a double tressure of the same, ensigned by a royal crown. These creations ceased in 1707.

BADGE OF
NOVA SCOTIA.

98

Dictionary of Heraldic Terms

KNIGHTS OF THE BATH. An ancient and honourable military order of knighthood. It was established in England by Henry IV., in 1399, who at his coronation created 46 Knights of the Bath, and revived by George I., in 1725. The chapel of this order is Henry VII.'s chapel in Westminster Abbey : the Dean of Westminster for the time being is always dean of the Order oᶠ the Bath. The number of the knights is according to the pleasure of the sovereign. At the close of the Peninsular War the Prince Regent, after-wards George IV., remodelled this order of knight-hood; and to enable himself to bestow marks of honour upon the naval and military officers who had distinguished themselves on the ocean and in the field, he divided the order into three classes. The first and highest are called Knights Grand Crosses of the Bath, who must be of the rank of major-general in the army or rear-admiral in the navy.

The second class is called Knights Commanders of the Bath; a great number of naval and military officers above the rank of captains in the navy and colonels in the army are admitted into this class.

The third class is styled Companions of the Order of the Bath, and is open to officers of inferior rank.

There has also been a civil division of this order since 1847.

KNIGHTS OF ST MICHAEL AND ST GEORGE. Instituted on 27th April 1818; is chiefly conferred on those who have rendered distinguished services in the colonies and in foreign affairs.

KNIGHTS OF THE ORDER OF THE STAR OF INDIA. Insti-tuted 23rd February 1861, this order is conferred on princes and chiefs in India, and on such other persons who have rendered important and loyal services to the Indian Empire.

KNIGHTS OF THE ORDER OF THE INDIAN EMPIRE. Instituted 31st December 1877, to commemorate the proclamation of H.M. Queen Victoria as Empress of India. Is conferred on the same classes of persons as the Order of the Star of India.

KNIGHTS OF THE ROYAL VICTORIAN ORDER. Instituted 21st April 1896, and conferred on those who have merited royal favour, and have rendered important services to the Crown.

KNIGHTS OF THE BRITISH EMPIRE. Instituted June 1917.

LABEL. The mark of cadency of an eldest son during his father's lifetime. See p. 24.

LAMBREQUIN. See MANTLING.

LANGUED. A term derived from the French word *langue*, tongue. It signifies in heraldry that the tongue of a bird or beast is of a different tincture from the body.

LARMES. Tears.

LION. The lion was early adopted as a charge in heraldry, and was appropriated by sovereigns and leading nobles for their arms. It thus appears in the arms of the kings of Scotland, Norway, and Denmark, and on those of the families Bohun, FitzAlan, and Percy in England, and Dundas, Home, Wallace, Dunbar, Lyon, and others in Scotland. The earliest example to be found is on the seal of Philip I., Duke of Flanders, in 1164. The following are the most

Dictionary of Heraldic Terms

usual positions in which the lion appears in shields of arms :—

Rampant.

Rampant guardant.

Rampant reguardant.

Salient.

Statant guardant.

Passant.

When the lions' heads are placed in the same position as in rampant guardant and reguardant, they are then said to be passant guardant and reguardant.

Sejant.

Couchant.

Dormant.

Manual of Heraldry

If two or more lions are introduced, they are supposed to be lion's whelps, or in heraldic terms lioncels.

Two lioncels addorsed or back to back.

Lioncels combatant.

Lion rampant double-headed.

A tricorporate lion guardant.

There are a number of other ways of introducing this charge. Many of them will be seen under the proper words that describe their condition, such as the word debruised, where the lion is confined by a fess or other charge passing over it; demi-lion, or half lion; but the examples here given will be sufficient to explain their positions, active or passive. They are introduced in arms of every metal and tincture known in heraldry.

LIVERY COLOURS. Are formed from the principal metal and tincture of the shield. When that tincture is gules, red being the royal livery, it is used in a duller tone by subjects.

Dictionary of Heraldic Terms

LODGED. A stag sitting on the ground with its head erect, is said to be lodged.

LOZENGE. A diamond-shaped figure, but not rectangular, two of its angles being acute and two obtuse. The arms of ladies are always displayed on a lozenge instead of an escutcheon.

Ex. Or, a lozenge vert.

LOZENGY. Covered with lozenges.

Ex. Lozengy gules and argent.

LUCY, or LUCE. A pike (fish).

LUNA. The moon: it formerly signified argent in emblazoning the arms of sovereigns.

LYMPHAD. See GALLEY.

MANCHE. An ancient sleeve with long hangings to it.

Ex. Argent, a manche gules.

Manual of Heraldry

MANED. When the manes of horses, unicorns, etc., are of a different tincture from their bodies they are said to be maned of that colour.

MANTLE. A long robe or cloak of state.

MANTLING, or LAMBREQUIN. The flowing drapery forming the scroll-work displayed on either side of the helmet from beneath the wreath, representing the ancient covering of the helmet, used to protect it from stains or rust. It is coloured from the principal tincture and metal of the shield, and is described as gules doubled argent, and so forth, in the cases of persons under the rank of peers. A peer's mantling is gules doubled ermine, and the sovereign's, or doubled ermine. For many years in Scotland it was customary to make the mantlings of all subjects gules doubled argent, but since 1891 the ancient practice has been revived. When the mantling incloses the escutcheon, supporters, etc., it represents the robe of honour worn by the party whose shield it envelops.

MARQUESS. The second order of nobility in Britain, next in rank to a duke. The title was first conferred in England in 1386 on Robert de Vere, who was then created Marquess of Dublin, and in Scotland in 1475-6 on James, second son of King James III., who was created Marquess of Ormonde at his baptism. The mantle of a marquess has three and a half rows of ermine on the cape, and his coronet is a circle of silver gilt surmounted by four gold strawberry leaves and four silver balls alternately, and a cap of crimson velvet, turned up ermine, and surmounted by a golden tassel. See p. 75.

Dictionary of Heraldic Terms

MARSHAL. Originally a farrier, but now a title of honour. See EARL MARSHAL.

TO MARSHAL. To place persons in due order, according to their precedency, in public processions, such as coronations, proclamations of peace or war, funerals, etc.

MARSHALLING ARMS. The disposing of several coats of arms belonging to distinct families in the same escutcheon, together with their ornaments, parts, and appurtenances. See p. 31 *et seq*.

MARTLET. An imaginary bird said to be without legs; it is used both as a charge and a difference for a fourth son.

Ex. Argent, a martlet gules.

MASCLE. An open lozenge-shaped figure perforated through its whole extent except a narrow border.

Ex. Argent, a mascle vert.

MEMBERED. A term used to express the legs of a bird when they are of a different tincture from its body.

MERCURY. The name of the planet, used by ancient heralds to describe purple in blazoning the arms of sovereigns.

METAL. The two metals used in heraldry are gold and silver, called or and argent. It is against the rules of heraldry to place metal upon metal or colour upon colour, unless for special reasons. Therefore, if the field be of any colour, the bearing must be of one of the metals; and, on the contrary, if the field be of one of the metals, the bearing must be of some colour. A well-known exception to this rule is found in the arms of Jerusalem—argent, a cross potent between four crosslets or.

MILLRIND. The iron plate placed on the top of a grindstone to protect the hole in the centre from the action of the axis; it is a charge frequently borne on escutcheons of persons connected with agriculture.

Ex. Argent, a millrind gules.

MITRE. A sacerdotal ornament for the head, worn by archbishops and bishops on solemn occasions. Certain English abbots formerly wore mitres, and they are frequently found as charges in the arms of abbeys and monasteries. The annexed is a representation of the mitre of the archbishops and bishops of the Church of England, borne as a mark of distinction over the arms of the see, or over their paternal achievements, when impaled with the arms of their see.

The Bishops of Durham were formerly princes of the Palatinate of Durham, and wore a ducal coronet surmounted by a mitre. They still retain the coronet and mitre as an heraldic distinction, borne over the arms of the bishopric.

Dictionary of Heraldic Terms

MOND. A globe encircled with a band and surmounted with a cross pattée; it is an ensign of royalty, signifying dominion.

MORION. A steel cap or helmet formerly worn by foot soldiers below the rank of gentlemen.

MOTTO. A word or short sentence inserted in a scroll, which is generally placed beneath the escutcheon in England; but in Scotland, unless in the case of a second motto, it is placed above the crest. The motto frequently alludes to the name of the bearer of the arms, as the motto of Lord Fortescue— FORTE SCUTUM SALUS DUCUM, A strong shield is the safety of commanders. Sometimes the motto is the watchword or war-cry in the battle where the original bearer won the honours that are retained by his descendants. Mottoes are not granted by the Heralds' College, but in Scotland they are always part of the achievement registered.

MOUNT. A mound placed on the base of the shield out of which a charge may issue.

MULLET. From the French word *molette*, the rowel of a spur: it is a star with five points, as in the annexed example; when more points are used the number is stated. It is sometimes pierced, when it is described as a spur revel.

Ex. Azure, a mullet or.

MURAILÉ. A French term for walled.

Manual of Heraldry

MURREY. A word used by ancient armorists instead of sanguine.

NAIANT. A French term for swimming. This term is used in heraldry when a fish is drawn in an horizontal position.

> *Ex.* Argent, a salmon proper, naiant, its head towards the sinister side of the shield.

NAISSANT. A French word signifying coming out. It is used when a lion or any other animal appears to be rising out of the centre of an ordinary.

> *Ex.* Or, from the midst of a fess gules, a lion rampant naissant.

NEBULÉ, or NEBULY. A French word, signifying cloudy, represented by a curved line, thus—

NIMBUS. The halo placed round the head of a saint.

NOBILITY. Under this denomination are comprehended in Britain—dukes, marquesses, earls, viscounts, and barons only. Archbishops and bishops are included in the rank of clergy. Nobility on the Continent means that a person is a gentleman of coat armour.

NOMBRIL POINT. That part of the shield below the fess point. See p. 17, letter F.

NORROY. The name of one of the kings of arms. See p. 11.

Dictionary of Heraldic Terms

NOWED. This word signifies tied or knotted, and is applied to serpents, wiverns, or any animals whose tails are twisted and enfolded like a knot.

Ex. Argent, a serpent nowed proper.

OGRESSES. Black roundels.

OPINICUS. A fabulous animal resembling a dragon in the fore part and wings, with a beaked head and ears, the hind part and four legs being similar to a lion, but with a short tail.

OR. The French word for gold. This tincture is denoted in engraving by small points. See p. 17.

Ex. Or, a bend gules.

ORANGES. Roundels tinctured tenné.

ORB. See MOND.

ORDERS OF KNIGHTHOOD. See KNIGHT.

ORDINARY. A term used to denote the simple forms which were first used as heraldic distinctions, and therefore called honourable ordinaries. They are the chief, pale, bend, fess, chevron, cross, and saltire. There are fourteen subordinate ordinaries, viz. : — Canton or Quarter, Inescutcheon, Orle, Tressure, Bordure, Flanche, Lozenge, Mascle, Rustre, Fusil, Billet, Gyron, Fret, Roundel. The form, size, and place that the honourable and subordinate ordi-

Manual of Heraldry

naries occupy in an achievement are all described in this Dictionary under their different names.

ORLE. Is a perforated inescutcheon composed of double lines going round the shield at some distance from its edge; it is half the width of the bordure.

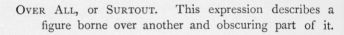

Ex. Argent, an orle azure.

OVER ALL, or SURTOUT. This expression describes a figure borne over another and obscuring part of it.

Ex. Quarterly or and gules, over all a bend vair.

PALE. One of the honourable ordinaries formed by two perpendicular lines drawn from the base to the chief. The pale occupies one-third of the shield.

Ex. Azure, a pale or.

PALL. A scarf in the shape of the letter Y, forming part of the vesture of a Roman Catholic prelate. It is introduced as the principal bearing of the Archbishops of Canterbury, Armagh, and Dublin.

Ex. Azure, on a pall argent, four crosses fitchy sable, in chief a cross pattée of the second.

Dictionary of Heraldic Terms

PALLET. A diminutive of the pale, which is one-half of its width.

PALY. A field divided by perpendicular lines into several equal parts of metal and tincture interchangeably disposed.

    Ex. Paly of four, argent and gules.

PANACHE. A plume of feathers set upright and borne as a crest.

PAPINGOES. Parrots or popinjays.

PARTY, or PARTED. Signifies divided, and applies to the several parts of an escutcheon parted by a line, which always runs in the direction of one or more of the honourable ordinaries, as may be seen in the following examples:—

PARTED PER PALE AND PER BEND SINISTER. Counter-changed, or and gules.

PARTED PER PALE AND PER CHEVRON. Gules and or, counter-changed.

Manual of Heraldry

PARTED PER FESS. A shield parted in the centre by an horizontal line through the fess point.

> *Ex.* Parted per fess, engrailed, argent and gules.

PARTED PER PALE. This signifies a shield parted by a perpendicular line down the centre, so that one shield may contain two coats of arms.

> *Ex.* Parted per pale, gules and argent.

PASCHAL LAMB, or HOLY LAMB. The badge of the Knight Templars.

> *Ex.* Argent, a lamb passant, carrying a banner charged with a cross. In Scotland the banner is that of the country.

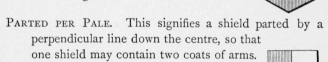

PASSANT. Passing or walking. See LION PASSANT and PASSANT GUARDANT.

PATONCE. See CROSS.

PATTÉE. A cross small in the centre, wide at the ends. See CROSS.

PATRIARCHAL CROSS. Cross used by patriarchs in the Greek Church. See CROSS.

PEACOCK. A peacock with his tail expanded is said to be in his pride.

PEAN. The name of a fur, the field sable, the tufts or. See p. 20.

PEARL. A precious stone, used by ancient heralds for argent in emblazoning the arms of peers.

Dictionary of Heraldic Terms

PEER. Name given to all persons included in the rank of nobility.

PEGASUS. A winged horse.

PELLETS, or OGRESSES. Black roundels.

PENDANT. A shield suspended or hanging from a branch of a tree, or from a nail. Shields of arms frequently appear drawn thus in architecture, and when described are said to be pendant.

PENNONS. Small flags borne at the end of a lance of an esquire or gentleman, bearing his paternal arms. The end of the pennon was cut off upon the person being created a knight banneret. See BANNERET. Penoncels or Pencils were small flags decorating the helmet or the horse armour. They are now only used at funerals. The large flag in the engraving is a pennon; the smaller, penoncels or pencils.

PHEON. A missile instrument with a barbed head, thrown from a crossbow. The head of a dart barbed and engrailed.

Ex. Argent, a pheon proper.

Manual of Heraldry

PIERCED, or PERFORATED. Cut through the centre.

> *Ex.* Argent, a mullet pierced, sable, on a chief azure, three mullets pierced, of the first.

PIETY. A pelican is said to be "in her piety" when seated on her nest and vulning her breast to feed her young.

PILE. An angular figure like a wedge, formed by lines running from the dexter and sinister chief to the middle base. It may also issue from the base or side.

> *Ex.* Argent, a pile purpure.

IN PILE. Arms or other charges that are placed so as to form the shape of a pile are said to be borne in pile.

> *Ex.* Argent, three swords in pile, points downwards.

PLATE. One of the six roundels; its colour is argent, but the tincture is not mentioned, as the plate is always silver.

PLENITUDE. The moon "in her plenitude" means a full moon.

POMEIS. Green roundels.

POMMELLED. The pommel of the sword is the round ball or knob at the end of the hilt.

Dictionary of Heraldic Terms

PORTCULLIS. A grating suspended by chains, used to defend the entrance to a castle. It was the badge of the houses of Tudor and Beaufort.

POTENT. The ancient name of a crutch: when the field is covered with figures like small crutches it is called potent; when the heads of the crutches touch each other it is called counter-potent. See p. 20, and also CROSS.

Ex. Argent and azure, potent and counter-potent.

POWDERED. See SEMÉE.

PRINCE. The title of Prince of Wales is usually conferred by special creation upon the eldest son of the British monarch. It is not a hereditary title. All other sons, grandsons, brothers, uncles and nephews, are called princes of the blood royal.

PRINCESS. Daughter of a sovereign. In Britain the eldest daughter of the monarch is called the Princess Royal; the others by their Christian names.

PROCLAMATION. A publication by the authority of the King. Proclamations of a new sovereign, of peace or war, or other matters of importance, are usually read by one of the heralds at the Mansion House and other places in the City of London, and at the Mercat Cross of Edinburgh; but in Scotland those of a new sovereign are also made at the Gate of Edinburgh Castle, Holyrood Palace, and the Pier and Shore of Leith.

PROPER. This word is used to denote that charges in an escutcheon appear in their natural colour.

Manual of Heraldry

PURPURE. The colour of purple, described in engraving by lines drawn diagonally from the sinister to the dexter side of the shield.

PURSUIVANTS. See p. 11 *et seq.*

QUADRATE. Square. See CROSS QUADRATE.

QUARTERED. A shield divided into four equal parts by a cross is said to be quartered. The quarter occupying the dexter chief is marked 1, or the first quarter; that occupying the sinister chief, 2; the dexter base, 3; the sinister base, 4; as in the annexed example. When a primary quarter is itself quartered, it is said to be counter-quartered, and is then called a grand quarter. Arms are quartered to indicate descent from an heiress, for dominion, or as an augmentation or special concession. See p. 22.

QUARTERED, or PARTED PER SALTIRE. A field divided by diagonal lines crossing each other in the centre of the field.

QUARTERINGS. An escutcheon divided into any number of squares is said to contain as many quarterings; they may be as numerous as the arms required. When a shield has a great many coats as quarterings, the same bearings should not be repeated, if possible.

QUARTER FOIL. A four-leaved flower.

Dictionary of Heraldic Terms

QUARTERLY. This term is used to signify that the shield is quartered. In describing the royal arms of the United Kingdom we should say: Quarterly, first and fourth gules, three lions passant guardant, or. Second, or, a lion rampant gules, with a double tressure of the same, flory and counter-flory. Third, azure, a harp or, stringed, argent.

QUARTER-PIERCED. See CROSS QUARTER-PIERCED.

RADIANT, or RAYONÉE. Any charge having rays or beams about it.

Ex. Argent, a fess sable, radiant.

RAGULY. Any bearing that is ragged, like the trunk or limbs of a tree lopped of its branches, is said to be raguly. See CROSS.

RAMPANT. Any animal erect, having one hind paw on the ground, the other three paws and tail elevated, head looking to the dexter, is said to be rampant. See LION RAMPANT.

RAY. A stream of light proceeding from a luminous body.

Ex. Azure, a ray of the sun issuing out of the dexter corner of the escutcheon. The lines on each side are not noticed.

REFLEXED. Curved and carried backwards.

REGUARDANT. An animal looking towards the sinister side of the shield. See LION REGUARDANT.

REST. The figure inserted in the illustration of the word "clarion" is by some writers on heraldry thought to represent a rest for a lance, and they give the charge that name. See CLARION.

RIBAND. A diminutive of the bend, being one-third less than the garter or bendlet, and never more than one-sixth of the field.

Ex. Gules, a riband or.

RISING. Applied to a bird about to fly.

ROUNDELS. Small round figures, all named from different metals and tinctures. See titles, BEZANT, FOUNTAIN, GOLPS, GUZES, HURTS, ORANGE, PELLET, PLATE, POMEIS, and TORTEAUX.

RUBY. A precious stone, formerly used instead of gules.

RUSTRE. A lozenge pierced with a circular opening.

SABLE. The term used in heraldry for black.

SALIENT. An animal springing forward. See LION SALIENT.

SALTIRE. One of the honourable ordinaries, by Scottish heralds called St Andrew's Cross, being a representation of the cross of his martyrdom. It is formed of two bands crossed diagonally in the form of the letter X. If uncharged it occupies one-fifth of the shield, if charged one-third.

Ex. Argent, a saltire gules.

SANGLIER. A wild boar.

SANGUINE. One of the heraldic tinctures. It is a dark red or blood colour. By some armorists it is called

Dictionary of Heraldic Terms

murrey. The latter word is considered obsolete. See p. 19.

SAPPHIRE. The name of a precious stone, formerly used to express azure.

SARDONYX. A precious stone, formerly used to denote sanguine in emblazoning the arms of the English nobility.

SATURN. The name of a planet, used to denote sable in emblazoning the royal arms by ancient armorists.

SCEPTRE. A royal staff; an ensign of sovereignty borne in the hand. It was originally a javelin without a head. Sceptres of the present time are splendidly decorated with jewellery. *The sceptre with the dove* is of gold, three feet seven inches long; the circumference of the handle is three inches, and two inches and a quarter at the end of the staff; the pomel is decorated with a fillet of table diamonds and other precious stones; in the centre is an ornament of enamel and gems, and gold open work with gems and diamonds; the mond at the top is enriched with a band of rose diamonds; upon the mond is a small cross of Calvary, over which is a dove of white enamel with its wings expanded, as the emblem of mercy, the eye, beak and feet of gold.

The royal sceptre with the cross is of gold; it is in length two feet nine inches, the fleur-de-lis of six leaves; the mond and the cross pattée above it are richly embellished with amethysts and diamonds. The upper part is wreathed; collars of gems and enamels enclose a smooth portion as a handle; and the foot is formed of rich sprays of gold and enamels jewelled with coloured stones and diamonds.

Manual of Heraldry

SCRAPE. A diminutive of the bend sinister, being half its size. It is seldom used in heraldry.

Ex. Argent, a scrape gules.

SCROLL. The riband above or below the escutcheon, on which the motto is inscribed.

SEEDED. When the seed of a rose or any other flower is of a different tint from the petal, it is called seeded.

SEGREANT. This term is used to describe a griffin or wyvern displaying its wings as if about to fly.

Ex. A griffin rampant, segreant, gules.

SEIZE-QUARTIERS are the arms of the sixteen great-great-grandparents of an individual.

SEJANT. French word for sitting. See LION SEJANT.

SEJANT GUARDANT. Sitting, but with head full faced, or affrontée.

SEMÉE. A French word for strewed. A field powdered or strewed with any object is said to be semée; thus a shield may be semée of fleur-de-lis, semée of hearts, etc.

SET FOIL, or SIX FOIL. Six leaves conjoined in the centre.

SHAKE FORK. A charge resembling the letter Y.

Dictionary of Heraldic Terms

SINISTER.   A term used in heraldry to signify the left side of any object; that is, the side on the right of the spectator.   Thus a bend proceeding from the top of the left side of the shield is called a bend sinister.

SINOPLE.   See VERT.

SLIPPED.   Torn from the stock or branch.

Ex.   Azure, three laurel leaves slipped, argent.

SOL.   A planet, formerly used to denote or in emblazoning royal arms.   It is the Latin name for the sun.

SOL, or THE SUN IN ITS SPLENDOUR.   The sun is said to be in its splendour when it is figured (that is, delineated with a human face) and surrounded with rays.   Sometimes this figure is called a sun in its glory.

Ex.   Azure, the sun in its splendour.

SQUARE-PIERCED.   Pierced with a small square orifice.

STANDARD.   A large narrow flag, bearing the whole of the achievements of the monarch or nobleman.   Those of the English had the flag of that country, the red St George's Cross on a white ground, next the hoist, and those of the Scots the white saltire of St Andrew on a blue ground, beyond which was emblazoned the badges and motto of the owner.   The royal standard, when placed before the pavilion of the monarch, either at a tourney or in an encampment, was eleven yards long and three yards broad.

Manual of Heraldry

The length of the standard, when borne in the field, denoted the rank of the leader. That of a duke was seven yards long; a peer of lower degree raised a standard five yards in length; that of a knight banneret was only four. In modern times standards of peers or knights banneret are seldom displayed but in funeral processions. The standard is then long and narrow, and pointed at the end; that of a duke is about fifteen feet in length; peers of lower degree about twelve.

The flag borne as the ensign of a regiment of cavalry is called a standard. The flags of foot soldiers are called colours, and are usually two in number, one being called the king's and the other the regimental.

STAR. This celestial figure is always represented as argent, and has six rays or points; if it has more points the number must be named. See ESTOILE.

STATANT. An animal standing still, with all its legs on the ground. See LION STATANT.

SUB-ORDINARY. See ORDINARY.

SUPPORTERS are figures placed on each side of the shield as if to support it. Supporters in English heraldry are granted only to persons included in the rank of nobility, or to knights grand cross of various orders under the statutes of the same. They are usually two in number, but single supporters occur occasionally. In England supporters are granted under royal warrant, but in Scotland Lyon has power to confer them on certain classes of persons who by custom have been held to be entitled to such. They are peers, the representatives of the minor barons who sat in parliament before 1587, chiefs of clans, gentle-

122

Dictionary of Heraldic Terms

men who can prove the immemorial usage from a period long anterior to the passing of the Act of Parliament, 1672, and persons on whom the sovereign has conferred the right by royal warrant. Baronets, as such, are not entitled to supporters.

SURMOUNTED. When a figure or bearing has another placed over it, it is said to be surmounted.

> *Ex.* Gules, a sword erect in pale, argent, surmounted by two keys in saltire, or.

SURTOUT. The French word for "over all." See ESCUTCHEON OF PRETENCE and OVER ALL.

TABARD. The official dress of officers of arms. See p. 13.

TALBOT. A dog formerly used for hunting. It is formed something between a hound and a beagle.

> *Ex.* Argent, a talbot's head erased, semée of billets.

TENNÉ, or TAWNEY. One of the tinctures used in emblazoning arms. It signifies orange colour, and is represented in engraving by lines drawn diagonally from the sinister to the dexter side of the shield, traversed by perpendicular lines from the base to the chief. See p. 18.

THUNDERBOLT is depicted by a twisted bar, inflamed at the ends, with wings, and having four forked and barbed darts in saltire issuing from its centre.

Manual of Heraldry

TIARA. The pope's mitre, with its triple crowns.

TIERCED. Is when the field of the shield is divided into three equal portions.

TINCTURE. A term used in heraldry to express colour. See p. 17.

TOPAZ. The name of a precious stone, formerly used instead of or in emblazoning the arms of the English nobility.

TORSE. The crest wreath.

TORTEAUX. Red roundels.

Ex. Argent, three torteaux in bend sinister.

TORTILLY. A description applied to an ordinary when wreathed.

TOURNAMENTS were combats of honour, in which knights entered the lists to gain reputation in feats of arms. The name is derived from *tourner*, to turn, from the horsemen turning frequently as they rode round the enclosure, and during the course of the engagement. The design of tournaments was to train the nobility to the use of arms ; none, therefore, were admitted to these sports but persons of noble birth, who could prove their descent, at least, by three generations. They were also required to be men of unspotted honour and integrity.

Dictionary of Heraldic Terms

The knights generally made their appearance four days before the combat. They endeavoured to excel each other in the splendour of their equipage and dress, and in the excellence and beauty of their horses, which were adorned with the most costly caparisons.

Their arms were lances of light wood, without iron at the top; swords without edge or point; in some instances wooden swords were used. The knights were formed into two parties, and entered the lists by different barriers, riding round the lists several times to pay their respects to their sovereign and the ladies. At length the quadrils, or troop, took their stations, and when the charge was sounded, the knights rushed against each other with the utmost impetuosity. The clashing of swords, the sounding shields, the war-cry of the knights, who shouted the name of their ladye-love in the midst of the mimic strife, greatly excited the spectators, who, in return, cheered and encouraged the combatants. When the knights were brave and determined, the contest lasted some hours; the vanquished, that is, those who were thrown from their horses, withdrew from the lists as quietly as possible, leaving the field to their successful opponents. The victory was decided by the number of knights unhorsed. The prizes to the victors were adjudged and delivered by the queen and the ladies.

Sometimes this entertainment was followed by jousts. Two cavaliers, out of gallantry, would break a lance in honour of the ladies. These were followed by others until the lists were again cleared for the tournament. The difference between tournaments and jousts was, that the former were in the nature of battles, the latter of duels.

Manual of Heraldry

When the sports were over, the heralds and pursuivants declared the names and titles of the knights, and proclaimed the heraldic ornaments which the emperor, king, or prince that presided at the tournament granted to those whom he pleased to reward or favour.

Notwithstanding all the precautions to prevent the mischief that might happen at these martial exercises few were exhibited in which a great number were not wounded, some killed in the *mêlée*, others crushed by the falling of the scaffolds, or trod to death by the horses. Kings, princes, and gallant knights from every part of Europe have perished at different times while attending or taking part in those mimic battles. Successive popes thundered out their anathemas against all that encouraged this warlike and dangerous amusement. Those who perished in these sanguinary entertainments were denied the honour of Christian burial; and yet, so strong was the passion of the nobility of Europe for these martial sports, that no bulls, decretals, or anathemas of the Church were able to restrain them. The use of gunpowder, and the consequent inutility of armour to defend the person in battle, gradually put an end to these animating shows. The tragical death of Henry II. of France, in 1559, who was accidentally killed in a tournament, caused laws to be passed prohibiting their being held in that kingdom. They were continued in England till the beginning of the seventeenth century.

An attempt was made to revive these martial exhibitions in Scotland by Lord Eglintoun, who proclaimed a tournament to be held at Eglintoun Castle on the 28th and 29th of August 1839. The

Dictionary of Heraldic Terms

lists were duly prepared, a covered pavilion was erected for the accommodation of the ladies, which would contain 3000 persons. In front of this pavilion was the throne of the Queen of Beauty (Lady Seymour) and her attendants. Around the lists, at convenient distances, were arranged the tents or pavilions of the knights, over which floated the gonfalon, or great banner, emblazoned with the arms and motto of the knight to whom the tent was appropriated. The knights vied with each other in the decoration of their pavilions; all was in accordance with ancient customs. The procession of the king of the tournament, the Queen of Beauty, with the judges, heralds, pursuivants, halberdiers, musicians, men-at-arms, as also the splendid retinues of the noble challenger and the gallant knights, presented a scene unparalleled for magnificence and heraldic emblazonment since the days of Edward IV. Unfortunately, the continued rain cast a gloom over this animated spectacle, which nevertheless excited the highest admiration of all who beheld it.

TRANSPOSED. Charges or bearings placed contrary to their usual situation.

Ex. Argent, a pile azure, issuing from the chief between two others, transposed.

TREFOIL. Three-leaved grass: the shamrock of Ireland.

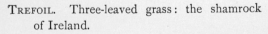

Ex. Argent, three trefoils gules, one over two.

127

Manual of Heraldry

TRESSURE. An ordinary not so broad as an orle. Tressures are frequently borne double, and sometimes treble, and are occasionally ornamented with fleurs-de-lis. The example contains only a single tressure. The arms of the King of Scotland exhibit an example of a double tressure flory and counter-flory. See DOUBLE TRESSURE.

TRICK is used to describe arms which instead of being emblazoned in the ordinary way are merely sketched in, and the colours indicated by abbreviations or signs.

TRICORPORATED. Three lions rampant, conjoined under one head, guardant, in the fess point. See LIONS.

TRIPPING. The motion of deer, between running and walking.

Ex. Argent, a stag proper, tripping.

TRUSSED. With closed wings.

TURBAND. In coats of arms, where the knight was a Crusader, this figure often appears. It was the form of the sultan's turban at that period.

TURRETED. A wall or castle having small turrets. In the annexed example the square tower has circular turrets at the angles, and is therefore said to be turreted.

Dictionary of Heraldic Terms

TUSKED. Any animal having tusks of a different tincture from its body is said to be tusked of that colour.

> *Ex.* Argent, a boar's head, erased proper, tusked gules.

TYNES. The branches of a stag's antlers.

UNDY. A term used to express the word wavy.

> *Ex.* Argent, a bend undy, gules.

UNGULED. When hoofs, nails, claws, or talons are of a different tincture from the principal charge.

URCHIN. A hedgehog.

URDY, or CHAMPAINE. See p. 22.

VAIR. A kind of fur formerly used for lining the garments of knights. It is represented in engraving by the figures of small bells ranged in lines, as in the annexed example. Unless the colour of the fur is named, vair is always argent and azure.

VAMBRACED. Clad in armour. Applied to the arms of the human body.

> *Ex.* Argent, three dexter arms, vambraced, couped.

Manual of Heraldry

VAMPLATE. The circular plate of steel fixed on a tilting lance to protect the hand.

VENUS. The name of the planet, used for the colour vert by ancient heralds, who emblazoned the arms of sovereigns by planets instead of metals and colours.

VERDÉE, or VERDOY. Semée of leaves or plants.

    Ex.   Vert, a bordure argent, verdoy of trefoils.

VERT. Green. It is represented in engraving by diagonal lines drawn from the dexter to the sinister side of the shield. See p. 18.

VISCOUNT. A title of honour, a degree below an earl, derived from the title vice-comes or sheriff of a county. It was first conferred in England in 1440, when Henry VI. created John, Lord Beaumont, to be Viscount Beaumont. The senior viscountcy in Scotland is that of Falkland, created 10th November 1620.

VOIDED. A term applied when any part of an ordinary is left open to the field.

    Ex.   Gules, a bend sinister, voided, argent.

Dictionary of Heraldic Terms

VOIDER. A subordinate ordinary occupying nearly the whole of the field.

    Ex. Azure, a voider argent.

VOLANT. The French word for flying. It is used in heraldry to express the same action.

VORANT. Swallowing or devouring : any animal, in a charge, devouring another creature.

    Ex. Argent, a serpent crowned or, vorant an infant.

VULNED. Wounded; used in emblazonry to denote an animal wounded.

VULNING. Any creature in the act of wounding itself.

    Ex. Argent, a pelican's head and neck, erased, vulning.

WALLED. A term sometimes used in heraldry, when an ordinary is edged or guarded by an embattled wall.

    Ex. Azure, on a pale, walled on each side with three battlements argent, an endorse gules.

Manual of Heraldry

WATTLED. Having a comb and gills like a cock.

WAVY, or UNDY. Curved lines, undulating like the waves of the sea.

> *Ex.* Argent, the lower half of the shield three bars wavy, azure.

WINGED. When the wings of a bird, or those of chimerical figures which are drawn with wings, are of a different tincture to their bodies, they are said to be winged. Thus, in the arms of the state of Venice, there is a lion sejant guardant, winged or.

WINGS DISCLOSED. When the wings are open, but pointing downwards.

WINGS ERECT. Wings are called erect when their long feathers point upwards.

WINGS INVERTED. When the feathers point downwards.

WIVERN. A chimerical animal, the upper part resembling a dragon, and resting on a tail nowed.

> *Ex.* Argent, a wivern, wings raised.

Dictionary of Heraldic Terms

WREATH.   A chaplet of two different-coloured silks
wound round each other, and placed on the top of
the helmet, to which and to the
crest it was secured by laces.   In
depicting a wreath below a crest
it should be shown as slightly
curved.   It is formed of the livery colours, which are
the principal metal and tincture of the shield.

CHAPTER VIII

HERALDRY may be considered as the symbolic history of
the royal, noble, and private families of Britain, from the
Conquest to the reign of Elizabeth; but it would require
a volume of far greater pretensions than this to enter fully
upon the heraldic history of even the peerage; which
assertion may be borne out by merely glancing at the
shields containing the arms of the British monarchs during
that period.

It was not until the reign of Richard I., about the year
1189, that the shield bearing gules, three lions passant
guardant or, became the cognizance of the English sovereigns.   Arms have been attributed to Edward the Confessor (azure, a cross moline cantoned with five martlets
or), and to the first four Norman kings (gules, two lions
passant guardant or); but there is no authority for these
Edward III., in consequence of his pretensions to be
King of France, quartered first and fourth the lilies of
France in 1340, and Henry IV. in 1405 changed the
field from semée of lilies to azure, three fleurs-de-lis or.
This coat remained unaltered till the Union of the Crowns
in 1603, when quarters were added for Scotland and
Ireland.   In England the arms were marshalled 1st and

4th France and England quarterly, 2nd Scotland, 3rd Ireland, till the union of the parliaments in 1707. William III., however, bore the arms of Nassau on a shield of pretence. By the Treaty of Union with Scotland the royal arms were to be such as Her Majesty Queen Anne should by order in council approve of. By an order of 17th

The Royal Arms.

April 1707 these arms were appointed to be as follows:— Quarterly 1st and 4th England and Scotland per pale, 2nd France, 3rd Ireland. On the succession of the House of Hanover in 1714 the arms of Hanover were placed in the fourth quarter. The arms were again altered at the union with Ireland by proclamation, dated 1st January 1801, to quarterly 1st and 4th England, 2nd Scotland, 3rd Ireland, over all in a shield of pretence Hanover, ensigned with an electoral bonnet, changed in 1816 to a crown. On the accession of Queen Victoria, the Kingdom of Hanover having passed to the Duke of Cumberland, the arms of that kingdom were deleted from the royal arms, and the present form came into use.

Supporters were not introduced in English heraldry previous to the reign of Richard II. The shield of this monarch is supported on each side by an angel habited, and beneath the shield by a white hart couchant, gorged and chained or, beneath a tree. The shield of Henry IV., the founder of the Lancastrian dynasty, was supported on the dexter side by a swan, on the sinister side by an antelope, both gorged and crined or. The shield of Henry V. was supported on the dexter side by a lion rampant guardant, crowned or; on the sinister side by an antelope, gorged and chained. Henry VI. had two antelopes as supporters to his achievement. The shield of the gallant Yorkist, Edward IV., is supported on the dexter side by a lion rampant argent, the tail passed between his legs, and turned over his back; on the sinister by a white hart, and in some instances by a bull. The supporters of the shield of Richard III. were two boars rampant argent, tusked and bristled or. Henry VII., as a descendant of the Welsh prince, Cadwalladar, assumed the red dragon as the supporter of the dexter side of his shield; the sinister being supported by a greyhound argent, collared gules. The shield of Henry VIII. was supported on the dexter side by a lion guardant, crowned or; on the sinister by a dragon gules. Edward VI. had the same supporters. Mary, on her marriage with Philip of Spain, impaled the arms of Spain and England as baron and femme; the dexter side of the shield was supported by the imperial

Heraldry in History, etc.

eagle, the sinister by a lion rampant, crowned or. Under
Queen Elizabeth the crowned lion rampant of England
resumed his place as the supporter of the dexter side of

The Royal Arms, as officially used in Scotland.

the shield, and the red dragon on the sinister. On the
union of England with Scotland, the supporters of the
royal arms in England were, on the dexter side a lion

137   s

Manual of Heraldry

guardant, crowned or; on the sinister, a unicorn argent maned and unguled or, gorged and chained of the same. The supporters of the royal arms have continued the same to the present time.

In Scotland these various arrangements of the royal arms since the Union of the Crowns have not been acquiesced in. Within that realm the arms, crest and supporter of the Scottish king have always borne precedence over those of the English, and this has been officially recognised by various orders by the sovereign in council approving of this form for use on the Great Seal and other official seals used in that country. It has further been enjoined by a recent order by the Secretary for Scotland for use by all government departments, and a special design for this purpose was prepared under the direction of Lyon King of Arms. The earliest use of arms by a Scottish monarch is found on the Great Seal of King Alexander attached to a charter, dated 1222, upon which appears a lion rampant within the double tressure flory counter-flory. In 1471 the Scottish Parliament passed an Act which, fortunately, was not acted on, ordering the tressure to be deleted from the royal arms, and in 1558 it was enacted that the arms of the Dauphin of France should be impaled with those of Queen Mary. By Act of Parliament in 1654 the arms of Scotland, viz., azure, a saltire argent, were ordered to be placed on the Great Seal in place of those of the king, which, however, were restored at the Restoration.

The first appearance of supporters to the Scottish royal escutcheon is to be found on the Privy Seal of James I. (1429), which is supported by two lions rampant guardant. The unicorn does not appear on the Great Seal till the reign of Queen Mary, 1555, but on one of the buttresses of Melrose Abbey, dated 1505, there is a tablet with the royal arms supported by two unicorns, and still earlier a single unicorn is found on the gold coinage of King James III. supporting the shield.

The Arms of the King of Scotland.

Ireland never having been a kingdom in the same sense as England and Scotland, did not have any arms until comparatively modern times. The harp, now used to represent

Manual of Heraldry

Ireland, was first introduced into the royal arms at the Union of the Crowns in 1603. It had previously, however, appeared on the Irish coins of the Tudor sovereigns, which, before that time, had borne the three crowns in pale, which had been granted by Richard II. to Robert de Vere, Duke of Ireland, as an augmentation to his arms. It was also carried at the funeral of Queen Elizabeth as the banner of Ireland.

The ROYAL BANNER, or, as it is more popularly and incorrectly called, the "royal standard," contains the four quarterings of the royal arms. No subject may fly this flag unless the king is personally present. In Scotland a practice has arisen in recent times of flying the old royal banner of the Scottish kings, in the mistaken idea that it is the national flag. This not only displays a lack of historical knowledge on the part of the persons who do so, but it is illegal, as it is the exclusive personal property of the sovereign, and a contravention of the Act of 1672.

The national flag of the United Kingdom is the UNION JACK, which may be flown by any British subject. It was first composed in 1606 by conjoining the flag of England (argent, a cross gules) with that of Scotland (azure, a saltire argent), the red cross of St George fimbriated white being superimposed on the Scottish ensign. As the Scottish people resented this placing of the English cross on the top of their flag, it was generally flown in Scotland with the Scottish saltire above the St George's Cross until 1707, when the Jack was declared to be the flag of Great Britain. On the union with Ireland in 1801 another saltire, supposed to be St Patrick's Cross, was conjoined with that of Scotland in such a manner that in the part next the hoist the Scottish half is uppermost, and in the other half the Irish one is so placed.

Heraldry in History, etc.

The white ensign, which is the flag of England with a Union Jack in the dexter canton, is the flag of the ships of His Majesty's navy and the royal yacht squadron, and should not be flown on land except at naval and coastguard stations. The blue ensign is assigned to certain government departments and members of royal yacht clubs holding an Admiralty warrant. The red ensign is distinctive of the mercantile marine. These three flags until 1864 were the distinguishing ensigns of the three squadrons (red, white, and blue) of the royal navy.

Heraldry had taken too firm a hold of the minds of the higher classes of society to escape the notice of the architects who were engaged by the sovereigns of England and by the wealthy barons to erect those splendid ecclesiastical edifices that still exist as the architectural gems of Britain. Westminster Abbey teems with heraldic ornament, not only in the chapel of Henry VII., but in those parts of the structure erected at a much earlier period. During the time when those styles of Gothic architecture prevailed that are now called the decorated and the perpendicular, the roof, the columns, the stained-glass windows, the seats, altar, tombs, and even the flooring, were filled with emblazonment.

Nor was heraldic ornament confined to architecture. It formed the grand embellishment of the interior of the palaces and baronial castles. The canopies of state, the furniture and plate, were all emblazoned with the arms of the royal and noble owners. And even at the present day, heraldry is far more effective for interior decoration than the unmeaning Italian scroll-work that is substituted for it.

One of the finest examples of the ornamental effect of heraldic decoration will be found in the recently erected

Manual of Heraldry

Chapel of the Knights of the Thistle at St Giles Cathedral, Edinburgh, and it is to be much regretted that owing to the smallness of the building the full scheme of decoration, by having the banners of the knights placed over their stalls, has had to be abandoned.

Numerous instances may be found, either in stained glass, monumental brasses, or illuminated genealogies, of female figures bearing heraldic devices on their apparel. A married lady or widow had her paternal arms emblazoned upon the fore part of her vest, which by ancient writers is called the kirtle, and the arms of the husband on the mantle, being the outer and the most costly garment, and therefore deemed the most honourable. This is called bearing arms kirtle and mantle.

In some of the later monumental brasses the arms on female figures are arranged differently; the arms of the baron appearing on the outside of the mantle, hanging over the dexter shoulder, the paternal arms of the femme on the lining of the mantle turned outwards on the sinister side of the figure.

PRINTED IN GREAT BRITAIN BY
OLIVER AND BOYD LTD.
EDINBURGH